HINTS

ON THE

FORMATION OF RELIGIOUS OPINIONS.

ADDRESSED ESPECIALLY TO

YOUNG MEN AND WOMEN OF CHRISTIAN EDUCATION.

BY

REV. RAY PALMER, D. D.,

Pastor of the First Congregational Church, Albany.

"Hold fast that which is good."—1 THESS. v. 21.

NEW YORK:

ANSON D. F. RANDOLPH, 770 BROADWAY.

1867.

This volume, when it was originally issued, was immediately republished in London and Edinburgh by the Messrs. Nelsons. The American edition has been for some time out of the market, and the present edition is from the English plates, which have been generously placed at the author's service by that respectable and well known house.

The very favorable reception of the book in all quarters, and the knowledge of particular instances in which it has been savingly useful, have lead to this new and corrected issue.

It is again commended to the attention of thoughtful young persons, in the hope that it may be blest of God to the confirmation of their faith.

R. P.

New York, *October*, 1867.

TO

JULIUS A. PALMER, Esq.,

OF BOSTON, MASS.,

WHOSE WARM FRATERNAL AFFECTION AND STEADY CHRISTIAN FRIENDSHIP, HAVE BEEN AMONG THE GREATEST BLESSINGS OF MY LIFE;

AND WHOSE

FAITHFUL LABORS AND LONG EXPERIENCE IN THE RELIGIOUS INSTRUCTION OF YOUNG MEN AND WOMEN

WILL ENABLE HIM

TO APPRECIATE THIS ATTEMPT TO AID THEM IN THEIR DIFFICULTIES,

THESE PAGES ARE AFFECTIONATELY

INSCRIBED

BY HIS OBLIGED AND GRATEFUL BROTHER,

RAY PALMER.

Preface.

THE following discourses are not addressed to positive unbelief. A different method would be necessary in order to the hopeful treatment of this. They were prepared for the benefit of those who, having been educated into a full belief of the Christian faith, have found themselves, on coming to maturity, or afterwards, disturbed with inward questionings and doubts. The design was, by hints in relation to some of the more important subjects, to assist such in giving their thoughts a right direction, and in confirming themselves intelligently in their early religious convictions. The reader will not expect to find in popular addresses the completeness of discussion which belongs to the class-room, but only such a style of treatment as the occasion and the special end in view demanded. In the present state of the popular mind, there are doubtless great numbers of the best educated young people of our country who, whether they avow it or not, are in the state of uncertainty and hesitation to which we have referred. To such it is hoped these pages may have an interest, and render some timely aid.

R. P.

Contents.

WHAT IS TRUTH?

I.

Evils of a State of Scepticism.

HEB. xiii. 9: *Be not carried about with divers and strange doctrines: for it is a good thing that the heart be established with grace.*

I HAVE been for some time proposing to myself to address to the congregation, more particularly to the younger portion of it, some thoughts on the formation of religious opinions. The vital importance of the topic as related to the present state of the popular mind, and the consideration that there is growing up among us so large a class of intelligent young persons, many of whom have enjoyed superior advantages of education, have seemed to render it specially proper that our attention should be turned in this direction. I am aware that a full and thorough discussion of the subject would involve the treating of some questions too abstruse and difficult for popular discourse; but without proposing to say all that such a discussion would require, it may at least be possible to give such hints as may be useful to the thoughtful and candid inquirer. This is what I shall attempt to do.

The importance to be attached to the forming of opinions, in any case, will of course be proportioned to the intrinsic moment of the matter to which they relate. The fact that we gather here from week to week is itself an acknowledgment that, in our judgment, the things pertaining to religion are things of the gravest import. It is a virtual avowal that we are convinced, at least in our understandings, that our religious responsibilities are most weighty and solemn in their bearing, our religious interests the most sacred and precious of all the interests of our being, and religious truth, of course, of all truth the most highly to be prized. Whatever directly concerns our characters and training as the responsible creatures of God and the heirs of immortality, does certainly demand our earnest consideration.

The present topic of discourse will be that which is naturally suggested by the text: the evils of an habitually unsettled and fluctuating state of mind, as compared with the fixed stability which rests on the solid foundations of truth, thoroughly examined and cordially received and held.

It would seem hardly to be expected, where ample means of religious knowledge are enjoyed, that such a state of mind should be a common thing. The habitual study of Christianity in its sacred records and in its practical results, from childhood up to adult years, would gradually, it might naturally be supposed, lead to a full and satisfying conviction of its truth, or else to the decided and conclusive rejection of it as a false and worthless system. The fact, however, it is certain is quite otherwise. Perhaps in nothing does the perverted condition of our moral nature more appear than in the inaptitude which men naturally exhibit to comprehend truths which are spiritual in their nature, and the difficulty with which they are brought to feel their reality, and to perceive their practical applications in relation to themselves. This want of susceptibility to the truths pertaining to God and religion, was recognised by Socrates and Plato, by Cicero and Seneca, as well as by Paul and John. Deism not less than Christianity has encountered and acknowledged it. It is, indeed, too plain to be denied. It is a fact that stands out in prominence on the history of the race, that the clearness with which the moral and spiritual truths which most concern men are perceived, and the strength of the impression which they make, are not at all in proportion, generally, to the evidence with which they are attended. Hence doubt very frequently exists where the materials of certainty are ample.

Of those who are educated under religious light and influence, and who are led in early life to accept Christianity, a very considerable number sooner or later find themselves to have reached a state in which they are disposed to question almost everything pertaining to religion. More commonly this crisis arrives in advanced youth, or on the verge of manhood. Up to that time the mind has been content to take as truth, on the authority of others, and with but little question, whatever may have been taught it. It has acquiesced, without serious difficulty, in the statements of parents and teachers as to what were the claims of duty; and has generally taken it for granted, however little it may practically have felt their power, that the views in which it has been trained to rest are sound. But now there comes a change. Of the views and impressions which childhood entertained on a variety of subjects, advancing years and knowledge have shown many to be erroneous. In respect to others, it is now perceived that although they may be true, they have been received without examination, and retained by the force of habit or authority, and not from an apprehension of the evidence by which they are made certain. It is not strange that such discoveries should beget a doubting spirit—a disposition to doubt even with as little reason and as little justice as was exhibited before in yielding an assent. In this state of mind the inquirer is inclined to question everything, as he once was to believe everything. He has found a few things, or, if you please, many things, to be false, and so he is afraid to believe that anything is true. He passes, by a not unnatural process, from the extreme of credulity to the extreme of scepticism.

No wonder that, in such a state of feeling, the truths of religion and its claims should come to be questioned with a greater or less degree of earnestness; and inasmuch as they make a strong appeal to the conscience on the mere statement of them, and aside from all proof, and also involve, if they are what they seem, the highest of all interests, it is only natural that the result should be an inward strife, perplexed and troubled thoughts, and a restless uncertainty of mind whenever these subjeets are considered. As an aggravation of the evil, too, it is just at this same period that the youthful heart begins to feel the temptations that solicit appetite and kindle passion, attracting to self-indulgence and the pursuit of worldly pleasure. It is perceived that religion speaks with a grave and earnest voice; that she commands self-discipline and self-restraint; that she forbids to make life a mere chase after selfish gratifications, and insists that great and difficult duties should be undertaken and laboriously discharged. Here, then, are reasons to the young just beginning to look out on life's illusions, for wishing that the teachings of religion may not, after all, be true; and the excited wish is likely to exert a powerful influence on the judgment, and greatly to increase the difficulty of weighing these teachings with candid impartiality. Between a doubting frame of mind and the drawing of inclination on the one hand, and the wants of the soul and the urgent power of religious truth, upon the other, the individual hesitates, and balances, and wavers, and seems to himself to be standing among shifting sands, where he can plant his feet on nothing that is firm.

At this point one of three things must happen: Either the mind must become utterly lost to truth, and settle itself on the ultimately fatal grounds of false opinion; or it must drift on unfixed, full of uncertainty, and driven now this way and now that on the troubled sea of doubt; or, lastly, it must lay hold of the strong cable of sound evidence, and intelligently and deliberately cast anchor on the sure foundations of the truth. There are doubtless some who do succeed in confirming themselves in falsehood beyond the chance of recovery. We are sure, also, that there are those who gain a hold on truth which nothing can relax, and which permanently sets their hearts at rest. But how large a number fall into the intermediate class, the class of perpetual doubters!—of unstable souls, who habitually live in the disastrous twilight of uncertain speculation, and are carried about by diverse and strange doctrines, always catching at a new absurdity to relieve the weariness of dwelling on the last; who, in short, are very much in the condition of Milton's fallen angels when they—

> "Reasoned high
> Of Providence, fore-knowledge, will, and fate,
> And found no end, in wandering mazes lost."

What can be more deplorable than this unnatural, this morbid bewilderment of the soul? A rational nature was surely never made to live in a realm of phantoms that for ever mock it by putting on new shapes. Such a state is, of all things, to be dreaded.

For, in the first place, it must needs be an exceedingly unhappy state. To all minds that have received even a moderate degree of cultivation, it is a source of positive pleasure to have, on all important subjects, clear views and well-defined opinions. The healthful faculties delight in reaching and grasping truth when excited to inquiry. They are gratified at being able to settle things with certainty. So, on the contrary, it is painful to the sound mind to grope about in the "everlasting fog"—to be threading backward and forward the mazy labyrinths of vague inquiry, which chases shadows and catches at emptiness, finding nothing solid on which it can rely. This, we say, is the constitutional law of the mind, let the subject about which it inquires be what it may.

But if the matter in question be one on the right understanding of which great consequences are depending, there must be, in addition to the doubtfulness, the pain of anxious apprehension. The fear of what calamities may, soon or late, result from failure to ascertain the truth, will often haunt the mind and mingle more or less with all its thoughts. Religion, it is clearly seen, if it be anything, is of the highest imaginable interest; and to miss the truth in such an affair, may, it cannot but be felt, involve irreparable loss, disaster that nothing can retrieve. Here is a most effectual cause of disquiet to the soul. How can a man have inward peace, when it is wholly uncertain, in his view, whether he is the offspring of an Infinite Mind, or of a blind chance; whether he has a nature essentially angelic, or is only a better sort of brute; whether he has any certain guide to duty, or is left to find it out by accident; and whether, if he survive the tomb, his happiness or misery will, or will not, be then at all affected by his present character and conduct? Rest content with such questions as these unsettled! A fool may —a man of reflection cannot. You might as well rest content on a stormy sea, when you know not whether your ship be sound or rotten; your chart and compass reliable or worthless; the hoarse murmur which you hear, the howling of the wind, or the roar of the surf that beats on the fatal rocks! Nothing but profound stupidity can give the mind that lives in a state of wavering uncertainty respecting the essentials of religion anything that really deserves the name of peace.

It is also evident, still further, that a state of chronic scepticism tends greatly to enfeeble both the character and the mind. There is a very common mistake on this point. It is no unusual thing to meet with those, more particularly among young men, who have the notion that there is something indicative of a superior mind in a state of doubt. They imagine it a mark of originality and penetration to be sceptical about those things which others confidently believe—to be starting difficulties in opposition to all opinions; and so they are led rather to cultivate an unsettled habit of mind, than to endeavour to escape it. But the truth is just the reverse of this. A really vigorous and healthful mind cannot be satisfied to continue long in a dubious state, when, as is true in the matter of religion, the materials for forming fixed conclusions are at hand. A strong mind presses on to a decision. It is content only when getting at results. A sceptical habit—observe I do not say a season of temporary questioning, but a chronic *habit* of doubting—most generally indicates a want of mental energy to lay hold of evidence and to appreciate its force; a lack of the strength of mind required in order to rise above the prejudices and biases that embarrass and tend to warp the judgment. It betrays an intellectual feebleness already existing and likely to perpetuate itself.

For when the mind has been allowed, and rather encouraged, to wander among the mists of doubt; to look rather after difficulties, than after proofs; it seems to become incapable of logical deduction and unsusceptible to the effect of evidence. Having accustomed itself to waver, it cannot, when it would, decide; or, if it has in any case decided, it cannot hold to its decision. What yesterday it examined and concluded to be true, it is to-day, just as much as ever, disposed again to question. There is a manifest enfeebling of the power by which the mind, when in a vigorous state, makes use of evidence to establish itself with collected firmness on the solid ground of truth. That it should be so results from well-known laws of mind.

It will also be true that in proportion to this loss of force of intellect, there will be likewise a loss of general force of character. He who is unable to decide with promptness, will not be able to execute with vigour. The habitual vacillation of the mind will be sure to exhibit itself in a feeble, time-serving, irresolute course of action. There is no class of truths which operates so powerfully in forming the whole character as religious truths. There are no motives which produce such energy of purpose as the motives which religious faith supplies. A state of habitual doubting therefore, while it tends, whatever be the subject, to infirmity of mind and character, must tend to this with special force and certainty when it is in relation to the essentials of religion itself that the habit is indulged. Live without any settled views in politics, in philosophy, in practical economy, and you will be a weaker man than you would be with fixed convictions in relation to those subjects. But live in dim bewilderment in regard to the great matter of religion, and the enfeebling influence will be felt in a far higher and more mischievous degree. It will make you vastly inferior, as a man, to what you would have been with a settled religious faith.

There is yet another evil result of the habit of mind in question. It is very liable to impair the *love* of truth, and to lower the estimate set on it by the judgment. Truth has been well defined to be "the reality of things." To know truth is to know things as they are. On knowing them in this manner, on having a right understanding especially of those things that directly relate to us, our highest welfare essentially depends. Nothing therefore, in fact, is so precious to us as truth. As Solomon has said—the merchandise of it is better than the merchandise of silver, and the gain thereof than fine gold. It is more precious than rubies; and all the things thou canst desire are not to be compared to it. God has, accordingly, given the mind an instinctive love for truth, a natural desire to know things as they are. It is this that prompts the inquisitiveness of childhood—the prying curiosity that desires to have all mysteries cleared up, and that presses inquiry often back to the very elements of thought. It is an important end of education to encourage and strengthen this desire, and give it a right direction; and observation and experience show that, in respect to many subjects at least, it is, on the other hand, capable of being weakened, and almost or quite destroyed.

It is found, for example, especially easy to repress the instinctive desire to know, when there is occasion to apprehend that the knowledge of the truth might be for any reason painful; and this is the case invariably in respect to sinful man when he inquires about religion. While on this, as on other subjects, he feels the natural desire for knowledge, there are conscious reasons growing out of his own character, which prompt him to resist this desire, and rather to shrink from full and certain knowledge, than to seek it. He is inclined to indulge himself in something. The question, Is it right? suggests itself. If he presses the inquiry, he may find himself obliged to deny his inclination; and he will be very likely for this reason not to press it. The appetite for truth may yield to the stronger appetite for self-indulgence which now has possession of the mind. In every such case, of course, the love of truth must necessarily be weakened. There will be less appreciation of its value than before; and if the oftener the love of truth is repressed for such a reason, the feebler it becomes, it must finally be destroyed. But this is what is happening all the while in the unsettled, wavering, and doubtful mind. The inclination to indulge in all sorts of curious speculations and even idle fancies; to wander round and round from one opinion to another without seriously attempting to settle upon any, resists and gradually overpowers the instinctive appetite for truth. Truth now loses her attractiveness. There is a growing insensibility to her inestimable value; and at last there comes an indifferent recklessness that cares but little whether it has the truth or not; and which is ready to adopt the foolish maxim—that it does not matter whether one's opinions accord with the reality of things or not. Great, inexpressibly great, is the mischief done, when the rational soul, in its constitution noble, is thus virtually divested of one of its highest and most glorious attributes. It is fallen and debased, indeed, when its inward longing after truth, and especially religious truth, is felt no more.

It remains only to say finally, that a state of sceptical uncertainty is attended with great danger as regards its last result. To doubt about anything is, of course, to admit the possibility that it is true. To doubt about the claims and obligations of religion is to allow that we are not sure that these are not founded in reality. But while those who are floating on the sea of doubt, confess, by their very uncertainty, that the teachings of religion may quite possibly be true, they are sure to act, in the main, as though certain they were false. So long, for example, as you doubt whether there be a God, you will act, almost with certainty, as though you knew there were none; that is, you will live to yourself alone. So long as you doubt whether the Bible be a supernatural revelation, you will allow it to have little if any more weight with you than if you certainly knew its claims to be unfounded; you will not suffer it to control you. So long as you doubt whether you are to live beyond the grave, you will demean yourself, for the most part, as though the contrary were the fact; you will confine your thoughts to the present life. And then, by the supposition, when you have lived and acted as though these things are false, they may, after all, turn out to be the great and solemn realities which they are believed by religious men to be. When you shall have wasted life and opportunities in urging difficulties, and asking curious questions, and indulging in speculative scepticism, you may, as your doubts imply, awake to the serious certainty that there is a God, that the Scriptures are divine, that your spirit is immortal, that life was a season of probation, and that eternity is the scene of righteous and unending retribution. We are not now asserting, let it be observed, that these things are indeed so; we are only saying that since by doubting, you concede that they *possibly* are true, even to your own judgment it must be clear that you run the tremendous risk of *finding* them all true, though you have lived as if they were all fiction. It needs no words to show that if you live as though the truths of religion were mere dreams, and it shall finally turn out that they are great realities, you are undone inevitably, and that for ever. This, then, is the amazing peril of resting in a dubious, unestablished frame. Even those who do this cannot but perceive that they run the hazard, the unspeakably awful hazard of a wretched, lost eternity. Religion and godliness, according to their view of things, hang trembling in equal balance. The side of religion may, they admit, preponderate; and if it does, they have made everlasting shipwreck of their souls! How much to be deprecated and dreaded is a position that involves continually the danger of a fall from which there is no recovery!

Here, then, are weighty reasons for regarding it as a very serious evil to be in habitual doubt in regard to the truths and duties of religion—reasons which make it appear in the highest degree desirable that the heart should be established. Of course it follows that nothing should be done by any thoughtful person to favour such a state, but that, on the contrary, diligent and resolute effort should be made to avoid, or to escape it. When in the gradual unfolding and progress of the mind, that questioning, inquiring period, of which we spoke in the beginning, comes, it is a most interesting and critical period in one's history. It need not launch one on a boundless sea of doubt; engendering the chronic, intellectual, and moral disease of scepticism without end. It may be, it ought to be, the season in which the mind, enlightened and well directed, obtains the mastery over prejudice and inclination; lays hold of truth with a clear understanding of its grounds, and finds in it so received an abiding test.

Do any of you, my young hearers, find the impressions of your childhood giving way, in some degree, so that you feel disposed to question them and to demand on what foundation they are based ? You see with what seriousness you should regard the crisis. Never, in all your life, has there been a time when you so greatly needed the counsel of your kindest, most faithful, and judicious friends. To listen now to the cavils of the scoffer ; to neglect calm, honest thought and careful reading; to indulge the affectation of singularity in your opinions, or the taste for idle speculation ; to please yourselves with the fancy that it is a mark of manliness to doubt ; is almost certainly to place yourselves in that permanently evil state which we have been considering. Such a course is worse than folly; it is madness such as words cannot express.

Yes! Believe it, my intelligent young friend—the poor way-faring man, who wanders homeless and friendless over the wide world, finding never a voice of greeting nor a resting-place in which he may take up his abode, is far—far less an object of compassion, than he whose *soul* is driven about perpetually in the chaos of confused and dubious thought, where all is dim and shadowy, and can find nothing that is stable; who as to the highest and most vital questions of his being, has established nothing, and positively believes nothing! Rather than suffer yourselves to slide into such a state, it were wisdom to suspend all other business, to shut yourselves up in the chamber of meditation and research, and to bend the undivided energies of your minds on this one work of reaching conclusions which will satisfy; and this with humble, earnest prayer to the Father of lights for that divine illumination without which spiritual things are never clearly seen by any of mankind. Never can you say that truth is beyond your reach, till you have thus done your utmost to discern and to embrace it, in simplicity and honesty of mind. When you have actually done this, you will not wish to say it. We say nothing now as to what conclusions you will come to, when you shall have done your whole duty in settling your opinions; but we do say, without any hesitation, that conclusions of some kind—sound conclusions—conclusions that will set your minds at rest—you will be sure to reach.

It must be so. No greater absurdity can easily be conceived, than that of supposing such a being as man, with an intellectual nature, whose instincts yearn for truth, placed in the midst of this grand universe of things, without the power to know with certainty so much as is essential to his welfare. No, rest assured you are not doomed to so miserable a lot. You can have satisfaction on all really vital questions, if you will. You may plant yourselves, if you will do it, where, though floods come, and the tempests beat, and the refuges of error are all swept away, you can stand calmly and in serenity of soul, and feel your foundations firm. Believe it—nay rather, make the experiment for yourselves, and know it with a happiness that cannot be described. There is LIGHT—and you were made to see it. There is REALITY—and you were made to find it. There is religious TRUTH—the very truth for which your soul is groping—and you, you may grasp the inestimable treasure, and make it your own blessed and permanent possession. Dread to live doubters, as you would dread a moral pestilence which was certain to prove fatal to your soul.

II.

Nature of Reasoning and of Proof.

1 THESS. v. 21 : *Prove all things ; hold fast that which is good.*

IT is the high prerogative of man's intelligent nature to discriminate between truth and error. This is tc be done by careful, honest, and patient examination, and by the application of the proper tests. When facts or opinions pertaining to any subject present themselves to our attention, it is not until they have been tried by the understanding and established by the decision of the judgment, that we can properly be said to know them. Having fairly weighed all things, we are then able to hold fast that which is good.

In referring to the evils of a permanent state of uncer tainty and doubt, we have insisted on applying the mind resolutely and with vigour at the outset to the work of settling itself on something with the least possible delay. In so insisting, we have assumed, what it seems to us against all reason to deny, that in matters so vital to our welfare as those which religion necessarily involves, substantial truth must be a possible attainment to sincere and diligent inquirers. It may be true that no assiduity, on our part, can save us from falling into some comparatively trifling errors; but certainly it must be possible to save ourselves from such as are fundamental in their nature

—such as will have an essential bearing on the highest interests of our being. Of what use, pray, are the rational powers in which we boast ourselves, if they will not avail us at least so far as this?

But in order to the right use of our faculties, and of our means of knowledge, in the pursuit of religious truth, it is indispensable that we distinctly understand what mode of reasoning, and what principles of evidence, are demanded in the discussion of the great themes of religion. A wrong impression on the mind as to the kind of proof to be expected, in order to the establishment of particular truths, is without doubt one of the greatest, and at the same time one of the most common sources of embarrassment to those who are seriously endeavouring to settle their religious opinions. Many such persons have never had their attention called to the nature of evidence; and have not been led to notice that different subjects require widely different kinds and degrees of proof, and even directly opposite methods of inquiry. From mistaken apprehensions as to these material things, they have been baffled in their earnest investigations when they should have arrived at certainty.

It is my present object, therefore, to explain the nature of the reasoning and the proof by which religious truth in general is established. If the topic seems abstruse, and requires some special attention to understand it, the vast importance of it practically in relation to religious inquiry, must be my apology for taxing your attention with it. I will try to make what I wish to say as clear as possible.

First then, I observe that there are two kinds of reasoning employed to establish truth. One of these is called demonstrative, the other probable, or moral. This distinction is not a mere refinement of the schools; it is founded in the nature of things, and may be comprehended by any person of ordinary understanding. Demonstrative reasoning starts with something which is known, advances with positive certainty at each successive step, and ends in a conclusion that is absolutely irresistible, commanding the unqualified assent of every person who understands the statement of the process. Moral reasoning, on the other hand, proceeds by adding probability to probability, until there is no more room for reasonable doubt; and, from the nature of the case, a given amount of moral evidence may produce very different degrees of conviction in the minds of different persons. It is a proposition in geometry, that the angles contained in any triangle, are together equal to two right angles. The proof of this is drawn directly from the nature of lines and angles as previously defined; and the certainty of the conclusion is the same to every person in the world who is able to comprehend the terms employed. This is demonstration. I am told for the first time that there was such a man as Julius Cæsar. I demand the proof. A variety of facts are adduced in evidence, which separately rest on different authorities, and some of which have more and some have less weight, when taken by themselves; but all together, they prove that such a person did exist beyond a question, though not beyond the conceivable possibility that the contrary should be true. This is probable, or moral reasoning. It does not start in premises, nor end in conclusions, which are certain in the very nature of things.

The two methods, then, are seen to be altogether unlike. The one determines what is necessarily true; the other what is true in fact. A demonstration is wholly worthless if it be not absolutely perfect. A course of moral reasoning, on the contrary, may have great weight although it involves many possibilities of error. In the one case, conviction is entire at every step of the whole process; in the other, it is gradually wrought as the argument advances, and becomes stronger and stronger the further it is carried, each fact or circumstance combining to establish the conclusion.

In the next place, it is important to be observed that moral reasoning may produce as strong conviction in the mind, as firm a belief of the truth to which it has respect, as that which is produced by demonstration. It is very far from being true that nothing can be received by the mind as certain, which is not shown to be necessary in the nature of things. If this were so, then there would be nothing certain to us, which requires to be proved at all, except the abstract truths of mathematics and geometry; whereas there are, in point of fact, a thousand things not in themselves self-evident, which we believe as surely as our own existence, and to which demonstrative reasoning cannot be applied. Indeed, in the determination of our conduct every day in the practical affairs of life, we are continually coming to conclusions and acting on them without the least misgiving, with as absolute certainty as the mind is capable of feeling, where moral evidence—the evidence of probabilities—alone is possible. Of course, if this be so, the fact that any particular truth does not admit of demonstration, by no means makes it certain that it does not admit of *proof*—of being established to the entire satisfaction of the mind. If this matter is not clearly understood, there will be continual embarrassment in the attempt to settle truth.

Let us illustrate, then, for the sake of clearness. You are a merchant. You go to the post-office, and take from it a letter to your address. You receive it with full conviction that it comes from your business correspondent at New Orleans. You are as sure of this as you are that two and two make four; and nothing can add to the strength of your assurance. But on what is this assurance grounded? You have not, and cannot have, the evidence of demonstration. Demonstrative reasoning, from its very nature, can have no application to such cases. Your proof is all of the moral, or probable kind. Your sure belief is produced by a combination of circumstances which, according to the laws of the human mind, have all the *force* of demonstration, while not one element of the thing is really involved. This an analysis will show you.

Your ship, we will suppose, was expected to reach her port at a certain date; this letter bears that date, and purports to give an account of her arrival. This is one circumstance. You put on board the ship a freight of hay; and also some special article, say a few barrels of choice fruit, as a present to a friend; and the letter mentions that these are all in good condition. Here is another authenticating item. You sent a verbal message by the master of the vessel to your agent—the letter clearly implies that this had been delivered. Your son went passenger on board, and the letter refers to him as well. You forwarded by the master an order that your agent should enclose to you a draft of a particular amount and tenor; the letter contains precisely such a draft. You are familiar with the handwriting of your agent; and you recognise this letter as like the rest. And finally, you have a private mark which he is instructed to place on every letter that he writes to you, and you find it as usual upon this.

What then can be more plain, than that this letter has absolutely conclusive proof of authenticity—proof as convincing to the mind as any demonstration in geometry. Yet this proof is all of the moral kind. It does not shake your confidence in the genuineness of the letter—not in the least—that there is a conceivable possibility that some one has found out everything relating to your vessel and your business, has acquired the handwriting and possessed himself of the private mark, and has written you a fictitious letter, which the real one of your correspondent may in some particulars contradict to-morrow, and has made you a present of the draft enclosed. All this *is* possible. But it is enough for you that the probabilities that such a combination of proofs should be found deceptive are infinitely small. There are a million to one in favour of the genuineness of the letter. You do not ask, you do not feel the slightest wish for greater certainty.

From this example, therefore, it is manifest that moral reasoning is not at all inferior to demonstration in power to convince the mind so that it shall rest with absolute and unwavering confidence in the conclusions it has reached. Whoever objects to the certainty of any fact or truth which is properly supported by such reasoning, because demonstrative evidence is wanting, objects without good ground; and only shows that he himself does not understand the nature and the laws of reasoning. Nine out of ten, yea, even a much greater proportion of all the particular things which he believes without a doubt, and on which he daily without any hesitation grounds his conduct, are believed on probable or moral evidence. This is true in the case of every one of us.

We advance then, in the third place, still another step and add, that the whole field of religious truth lies without the circle of things which admit of demonstration. In other words, demonstrative reasoning, in its strict sense, as we have defined it, has no possible application to those subjects with which religious faith is properly concerned. We do, indeed, in the examination of these subjects, sometimes resort to the form of demonstration; but when we do this, we always start from premises which rest on moral proof; and so at last, it is on the certainty of moral proof alone that our conclusions stand. Moral reasoning would not be more entirely out of place in an astronomical calculation, than demonstrative reasoning would be in an attempt to settle a primary doctrine of religion.

We may refer, for the sake of illustration, to the being and attributes of God. We know of but one serious attempt to demonstrate the truth on this great subject—that of the celebrated Dr. Samuel Clarke; and this, although displaying great metaphysical acuteness, is universally regarded as a failure. The fatal difficulty is that the premises which he assumes as necessary truths are not such; or, in other words, the very nature of the subject renders the application to it of such a mode of reasoning impossible. Instead, therefore, of demanding a demonstration of the existence and attributes of the Deity, the inquirer who understands the true principles of reasoning will look for moral evidence; and if he perceives that there is such a kind and amount of moral proof as must, when properly appreciated, give a certainty beyond all reasonable doubt, he will ask for nothing more.

Let it be supposed then, that on looking for proofs of the divine existence, you find the following facts :—

First, that the notion of God, of divinity as one or many, is universal among mankind; as though it were to the human soul a necessary notion. Next, that when the reasoning mind sets itself to reflect upon the subject, it finds along with the consciousness of its own existence, the consciousness also that it is not self-existent, and a conviction that there must be a self-existent being on whom it is dependent. Further, that in both body and mind there are found clear indications of adaptation and design; that the eye is exquisitely constructed in relation to the light, the ear as curiously adjusted to the atmosphere, and every sense and every organ throughout precisely fitted to its purpose; and that the body, as a whole, is admirably suited to the entire necessities of material existence. Then as to the mind, suppose, that it is observed to have just those instincts, susceptibilities, and powers that are demanded by the sphere in which it is ordained to move, and appears to be in its capabilities of thought, affection, and volition, a wonderful product of creative wisdom; and that in the fact that it has a conscience, and an ineradicable sense of moral obligation, it seems to stand related to law, and of course to a lawgiver. Suppose still further, that without itself, the intellect perceives the universe as not self-existent, though in fact existing; that nature in every part offers indications of a well-adjusted plan; that each particular object exhibits nice contrivances which fit it to sustain its own existence, if endowed with any kind of life, to answer its special end, and at the same time an obvious relation to the great system of which it forms a part. And finally, suppose that the gradations of animal and vegetable life, the general order, harmony, and beauty in the entire arrangement of the whole, is such as to give the conception of an impressive unity in the midst of an endless variety and multitude. It appears as one grand universe, to compose which an inconceivable number of separate parts, or objects, harmoniously conspire.

Whether these things actually *are* as now supposed, we may inquire hereafter. We only say for the present that if you should find them so; and if in the presence of such facts, your soul should acknowledge and even imperatively demand a God, it would not disturb you that you had not a demonstration of the existence of a necessary infinite and eternal Being. You would have a moral argument carried to such a height of conclusiveness and strength, that it would be difficult to see how its convincing power could be increased. You would be in substantially the same condition as on the reception of the letter in the case already imagined. A million to one, as in the other instance, you must say within yourself, there is a supreme intelligent Cause, a God, as the Author of the universe; and yet you would be perfectly aware that there was nothing of demonstration in the case. You would not only feel no need of such a thing, but you could not help perceiving that the nature of the subject utterly forbade it. Where the proofs are all moral, the reasoning must be moral. There are no postulates or axioms in relation to the existence and attributes of God on which a course of demonstrative reasoning can be based.

In like manner the question of divine revelation may be seen not to belong to the province of inquiry within which the demonstrative method can properly be applied. No definitions, no first truths, or known relations of things, can possibly be laid down on which to reason with mathematical precision here. It requires but a moment's thought to see that to expect or to demand that a revelation, if made, should be supported by evidence of this sort, would be to demand what, in the nature of things, is impossible and absurd. You must, indeed, have proof—in a matter of such moment, proof of the most conclusive and satisfying kind, in order to believe; and if you find it at all, it must be in the moral form, one item added to another till there is no longer room for reasonable doubt.

Look at the case as it lies before the mind of one who after examination believes the truth of the Christian revelation. He starts with what he deems the obvious need there was that God should reveal himself to men, and the extreme improbability that the infinitely Good and Wise would create a being with such endowments as those that belong to man, and then abandon him to helpless ignorance in respect to the highest relations and the most important interests of his being. He finds next a professed revelation, appearing worthy to have come from God and exhibiting in its contents marks of a superhuman origin, claiming to have been received by special divine communications, and professing to be sustained by the evidence of various prophecies and miracles. In support of these claims he brings together the historic testimony to the truth of the sacred records in which it is delivered; the purity of its teachings and the grandeur of its disclosures; its adaptation to the great wants of the human race; the wonderful character, life, death, alleged resurrection and ascension of the Founder of Christianity, the entire spirit and character of the gospel as forbidding the supposition that it originated with wicked men; its early successes and its permanent power and progress in the world; its elevating influence on individual and social man whenever and wherever heartily received; the celestial peace both for life and death which it has been found to carry to the heart, and finally its immeasurable superiority to all other religions. It is, I say, with all these and various other similar items, that the believer in revelation constructs the argument on which he rests; an argument rising, as he thinks, with the force of a mighty accumulation, to a degree of certainty that leaves nothing to be desired in order to complete conviction. While the lack of proof would, of course, be fatal, the lack of demonstration, it is plain, is only the lack of something that has no possible relation to such a matter.

We need not refer particularly to other related truths of what is called revealed religion. The whole circle of spiritual doctrines, such as the Trinity, the incarnation, the atonement, the mission of the Holy Spirit, and others connected with these and resulting directly from them, so obviously belong to the sphere of moral reasoning, that the attempt to demonstrate them would be absurd, and of course to ask for demonstration is unreasonable and weak. If you assume the existence and attributes of God as proved by moral reasoning, you may, indeed, deduce in a demonstrative way from these as premises, some other important truths respecting him; and if on the same grounds you accept revelation as established, you may apply, in a qualified sense, the demonstrative style of argument in the determination of its particular doctrines. But in each case, since the premises rest on moral evidence, the certainty of the conclusions to which you are conducted will rest of course on moral evidence. Such are the laws of reasoning. Such is the unalterable nature of things.

We have only to add lastly, that the power of moral reasoning to produce conviction depends very materially on the state of the mind to which it is presented; while the power of demonstrative reasoning does not depend on this at all. Of course we mean the state of the mind as to its dispositions, prejudices, and biases of every kind. This is a most essential point of difference between the two modes of settling truth, and must not be overlooked.

Address the demonstration of a geometrical problem to any person who is competent to understand it, and no preconceived opinion, no aversion to the truth or wish that it should be otherwise, no unwillingness from any cause to be convinced, did these exist in ever so great strength, can make the smallest difference as to admitting the conclusion. The admission of it is absolutely and in the strictest sense *compelled.* The mind has no power to hold back or to evade; it *must* believe, or lose its rationality. But the case is widely different when you essay by moral argument to lead a person to a conviction of any truth. In this case, as the process advances not from the necessary to the necessary, but from the probable to the probable, there is room, at every step, for the influence of personal feeling and partial judgment, and aversion to the truth, to affect the force of proof to a very great degree. That, in fact, it does this often, is a matter of familiar observation. Moral evidence can have its proper force only when the mind is open, fair, and honest; when divested of all prejudice, and truly willing and desirous to follow in the track of evidence, and to accept the results to which it leads. Go to a young man who has acquired a love for the exhilarating glass, but as yet does not indulge to inebriety. Convince him of the danger of his habit—of the moral certainty there is that, sooner or later, his course will bring him to a dishonoured grave. To offer him abundant proof that his path directly leads to such a termination, is the easiest thing imaginable; but actually to convince him, is on the contrary one of the most difficult. His appetite, his inclination, his habit already formed, so blind and pervert his judgment, that your reasoning, conclusive though it be, is powerless upon him. Go to a person who is dishonest in his dealings, and daily puts in his pocket the gains of secret fraud. Repeat to him the adage that honesty is the best policy, as well as a high duty, and exhibit to him the proof. Your reasoning is sound and perfectly conclusive; but with him it has no weight. He is under influences from the course of conduct he pursues, which indispose his mind to receive conviction, and which really neutralize the power of evidence. So it may be in a thousand cases, so it may be in regard to all the great and vital questions of religion. Just so far as the mind, in its reasonings on these, is swayed by anything besides the love of truth; just so far as it is indisposed by any opinion, passion, or wishes of its own;—just so far it is unfitted to appreciate the moral reasonings by which they must of necessity be decided. It may be, therefore, it is plain, that the fundamental truths of religion are, in fact, sustained by the highest and most decisive moral evidence, and yet some persons may be in such a state of mind in relation to these truths, that, to them, this evidence shall be ineffectual and nugatory. Those who are in a state of mind to see and appreciate the proof, may rest in them a well-established faith, while these, like men groping with shut eyes at noon-day, may be dark and bewildered in their scepticism.

I have thus endeavoured to explain the nature and laws of reasoning, so far as the general object we have in view demanded. We have seen that there is an essential difference between demonstrative and moral reasoning, which limits the application of each to a certain class of subjects; that moral reasoning may bring the mind to sure conclusions, no less than demonstration; that the great questions of religion do not admit of demonstration, but fall wholly within the sphere of moral proof; and, finally, that the force of this sort of proof will necessarily be very much affected by the state of mind that prevails at the time it is considered.

The most important practical bearing of these views on the forming of religious opinions, will be shown in the following discourse. There is not time to enter on it now. I will simply ask you, in closing for the present, to consider a moment how much is necessarily involved in the work of forming your opinions rightly on the momentous subjects pertaining to religion. It is to be feared that too many young persons, even among the more intelligent, have little conception how great a work it is, and how much serious, careful thought and earnest application of the mind is needed to accomplish it. Many of you, perhaps, have never once imagined that you had much to do in relation to the matter. You have had a vague impression, not improbably, that the whole affair was of course to be left to time and chance; and that you had only to wait till you would see what these would bring. But if it is true, as you now cannot but perceive, that there is need of clear and accurate views as to the laws of reasoning, and of careful discrimination in applying them; if the mode of settling truth demanded by religious subjects, is that which supposes alike the highest activity and the best preparation of the mind,—then the task you have on hand is great and arduous, and must be very seriously attended to, or it will not be accomplished. If your mind is filled with questionings, you will not get permanent relief, without serious and earnest thought, the use of such helps as may lie within your reach, and especially an honest, heartfelt, daily application to the Fountain of all wisdom, for divine illumination. It is always an unfavourable symptom—alas, how often it appears!—when, along with a state of doubt, there is seen an indisposition to sober and candid inquiry, and a want of seriousness and prayerfulness of mind, and unmistakable signs of a prejudiced, uncandid temper. Truth will not reveal herself in her divine simplicity and beauty, her impressiveness and majesty, to those who have so little appreciation of her worth.

Does it seem to any of you too great a task to search for divine wisdom in the way which has been indicated? Are you unwilling to take the trouble to explore for yourselves, if doubts assail you, and that with an honest mind, the ground on which it is safe for you to rest? Are you inclined to save yourselves the pains of fair examination, to give ear to the specious suggestions of those who manifest an earnest desire to overturn the religious opinions which have been cherished by the best and wisest of mankind, and which have inspired their souls for noble deeds, and have blessed them richly with inward peace, not only living, but even in death itself? The main truths of the Christian religion have undeniably stood unshaken against all attacks for near two thousand years. This, of itself, affords a strong presumption that they are true, and is sufficient to justify you in refusing to accept, without the most thorough inquiry, the often superficial cavils of those who would reject them. It is certainly reasonable to look to the bottom of the matter if need be, and not to give them up without the most decisive reasons.

Nor should any labour which may be needful in order to reach the truth in matters of religion appear excessive. What! Is not your rational nature the grand distinction of your being? Is not the pursuit of truth, especially the highest and most spiritual forms of truth, the most worthy, the very noblest employment of such a mind as yours? Besides, what has become of those, in general, who have been content, in indolent neglect, to leave their religious views to be moulded by accidental influences? They have fallen, by thousands, into the miseries of perpetual doubt, and by thousands have perished in the inextricable entanglements of error. There is no safe alternative. You must learn the right mode of reasoning and apply it, you must read and reflect, not only with diligence and patience, but with a genuine honesty of mind; or you cannot enjoy the pleasure and the peace of resting in clear views, with an abiding satisfaction, but must run the dreadful hazard of dying in the wilderness of falsehood and delusion.

Can it be that there is one of us, who is so slothful and senseless as not to be stirred by such considerations—who will not think it worth his while to reserve a portion of those hours now given to trivial reading and fruitless thought, to be devoted in good earnest to the right study of religion? You will, of course, if you are wise, obtain judicious counsel for the shaping of your inquiries, so far as you may need it; but you will feel that you have personally a work to do. How *can* you be content, you especially whose eyes are glowing with the hidden fires of youth, and who feel in your bosoms the throbbings of an inextinguishable life, till you are fully satisfied, if you have been in doubt, whence you came, whither you are going, for what you have a being, and which of all the paths about you is for you the path of happiness and duty? Attain a sure foundation in the great matter of religion, and the infinite advantage will be yours. Neglect or fail to do it, and the darkness, the perplexity, the anguish which will ultimately come, it must be for you in your own persons to endure, without relief and without a comforter. Prove all things—hold fast that which is good!

III.

Responsibility of Men for their Opinions.

JOHN iii. 18: *He that believeth on him is not condemned; but he that believeth not is condemned already, because he hath not believed in the name of the only begotten Son of God.*

EVERY reader of the Scriptures is aware that belief in Jesus Christ, and in those essential truths which stand in immediate relation to human duty and happiness, is there continually insisted on as an imperative duty. It is so exhibited in the passage just recited. This is the work of God, said our Lord himself, that ye believe on him whom he hath sent. He that believeth shall be saved; but he that believeth not shall be damned. Of sin, because they believe not on me; as though their unbelief were the very sum and essence of their sin.

To say nothing now of the divine authority of the Scriptures, we may observe that their style of teaching in reference to the duty of believing what may be known as true, is not at all peculiar. Every eminent moralist, whether of ancient or modern times, whether in name a heathen or a Christian, has taught the same doctrine as to the duty of accepting the primary truths of religion and morality; those truths, that is, in respect to which the attainment of satisfactory conclusions was to be deemed a practicable thing. It is a remarkable fact, certainly, and one worthy to be specially considered, that the wisest and most candid men of all ages and all nations, when they have addressed mankind with a view to their improvement, *have* with one consent assumed that the act of believing, of assenting heartily to such moral and religious truths as are or may be known, is a matter of positive and solemn obligation—something which men are bound, and may be authoritatively required to do. It would seem that a thing so generally admitted to be true, and that by the soundest and most thoughtful minds, must be in itself nearly or quite self-evident, or at most, must admit of easy proof.

Notwithstanding, however, this so general agreement among the best teachers of mankind, there are many who are unwilling to allow that belief can be a matter of obligation, and unbelief a ground of blame. This, indeed, is one of the most common subterfuges to which those who are avowed rejectors of revealed religion, and whose lives are at variance with its precepts, have been wont to betake themselves. The well-known case of Lord Byron affords an example in illustration. The wife of an English clergyman saw his lordship at a place of public resort, and filled with admiration of his brilliant powers, was very deeply affected at the thought of their perversion. Not long after, she died; and her husband, on looking over her private papers after her decease, found among them a copy of a most simple and pathetic prayer in behalf of the noble poet, in which she entreated that he might be enlightened and guided from above, and learn to consecrate his extraordinary gifts to God. The husband enclosed this prayer in a letter to Byron, then at Pisa. For the moment it obviously touched his heart; and his acknowledgment of it is at once one of the most beautiful and one of the most creditable things he ever wrote. He evidently felt the reality and the worth of such a piety as that exhibited by the interesting stranger who had in secret breathed out to Heaven for him so pure and fervent a supplication; and he frankly confessed that the Christian believer had reason to be of all men most blessed. To this confession, however, he adds immediately, "But a man's creed does not depend upon himself. Who can say, I *will* believe this, that, or the other?" This is the ground on which he rested his defence of his unbelief and its practical consequences, as exhibited in his life. He persuaded himself that he had *no responsibility for his opinions.* It was no fault of his, he thought, that they were adverse to the Bible and its truths. He was merely passive in the matter. He could not change his views by an act of will.

We cannot better represent a class than by this particular example. We are almost daily hearing the same apology for doubt or error urged,—we are not responsible for our opinions. We *cannot help* believing as we do. We *must* believe according to the evidence we have. This, too, is said with apparent sincerity and confidence, and as if it admitted no reply. My present purpose is to examine the validity of this apology. In order to do this, let us look into it a little, and see what it assumes.

It is plain, in the first place, that those who assert that they are not responsible for their opinions, assume it to be true that conviction in regard to religious truths must be *compelled;* in other words, that the certainty of these truths must be carried to the mind by evidence that is literally irresistible, or else they cannot be believed. They take it for granted that the law of belief is as simple and invariable in its action as the law of gravitation. Attraction drives the body to the earth, without the smallest influence of any choice, or the least room for any responsibility on its part; evidence drives the mind to fixed conclusions by a like invincible necessity, and with the same absence of purpose or of will. Such is the view they take.

But the truth of the matter is, that whatever of plausibility there may be in this assumption, arises from the confounding of things that differ. It is plain that those who make it, either designedly or through ignorance and want of discrimination, confound entirely the two widely diverse kinds of reasoning by which truth in general is established, each having its own appropriate and exclusive sphere, and being limited to a certain sort of truths. These two dissimilar kinds of reasoning, you will remember, we endeavoured in the last discourse to distinguish clearly from each other. In taking it for granted that evidence in all cases must carry the conviction of the mind with the force of a felt necessity, the persons in question take it for granted, quite contrary to the fact, as we have seen, that all valid reasoning is demonstrative, and that no proof is conclusive except that which carries the mind, with certainty at every step, to a result which is absolutely necessary. It is indeed true, that in the reasonings of the mathematician, if the process be correctly carried forward, the steps are certain and the conclusion irresistible; but this sort of reasoning, it was shown, is applicable only to the relations of numbers and of quantity, not at all to the truths of religion. To these last, as was explained, moral reasoning alone can rightly be applied, in which, although complete conviction may be reached, there is *neither* certainty in all the steps, nor necessity in the conclusion. Let but the nature and the laws of reasoning, therefore, just be clearly understood, and it is seen at once to be wholly false that conviction in relation to moral and religious truths must be compelled, in a literal sense, and without regard to the particular state of the mind itself. No religious inquirer has any right to ask or wait for a kind of proof which is incompatible with the nature of the subject. Whoever does this clearly shows that he himself is either disingenuous and without an honest desire to learn, or else so careless as not to have considered what evidence he ought to look for. Lord Byron very well knew that he, and all men, daily formed conclusions the most positive and satisfying, and that where great interests were at stake, without anything like the evidence of demonstration—the evidence that must produce the same conviction or certainty in every mind, when rightly apprehended. He might have known, had he properly reflected, that all he had a right to ask was a sufficient amount of the same sort of evidence on which he acted in settling practical truth in the common affairs of life. He either imposed upon himself, therefore, or wished to impose on others by an insincere and sophistical evasion. The same must be true of all who attempt to stand upon the plea that belief can come only by irresistible necessity.

The assertion that men are not responsible for their opinions assumes also, in the next place, that passion, prejudice, and personal inclination and desires, have no influence on the reasonings and judgments of the mind, or else, that there is no responsibility attached to the existence of these affections.

But is it true that the mind cannot be biased in its inquiries by its own passions, prejudices, and wishes? Will any one seriously maintain a proposition so utterly at war with every day's experience and observation, when once it is distinctly stated? Take the case of the miser, for example. Why is it so difficult to convince him that it is more blessed to give than to receive? Is it that evidence is wanting of the essential meanness and the belittling effects of avarice? Or is it that he is blinded by a passion that has gained full possession of his heart? You have an enemy. Bring him, if you can, to do full justice to your character and conduct, in those particulars in which all others acknowledge them to be worthy of commendation. What is the difficulty? His bitterness of heart, like stained glass that colours all the landscape, allows him to see you only in false lights. It leads him to prejudge whatever you say or do, and to condemn without inquiry. Your child comes to ask of you some indul gence on which his heart is set. Your judgment and experience decide at once that it is not proper to allow it. Is it, then, easy to convince him? Will he weigh impartially your objections, with his own wishes on the other side, and pleading urgently against you? A villain is about to commit a robbery or a murder. There are a hundred chances against one that he will be detected and made to suffer punishment. How but through the deluding influence of his own desires and hopes, does he persuade himself that the chances are greatly in favour of escape? So in a thousand cases that will readily occur. If there is anything in respect to men that is daily exemplified and universally admitted in the common affairs of life, it is this fact—that clear, convincing, ample evidence, on any subject, is likely to avail but little, when addressed to a mind whose prepossessions, feelings, and desires, are all against it. There is sure to be a bias, in such circumstances, that is nearly or quite invincible.

But since all this must be admitted, it will possibly be said, that for these states of their feelings and their wishes, men are not to be held responsible, whatever their practical influence may be. It may be urged that every man is what he is, by the laws of his being, and by the force of circumstances; and that the various biases which affect the action of the mind, are therefore to be regarded as inevitable—a misfortune and not a fault.

Pray, what then has become of man's voluntary nature? Or in what sense is he an accountable creature and worthy of blame or praise? If a person's ruling passions, his habitual dispositions and desires, are not essential elements of moral character, in what does character essentially consist? If these do not depend for their existence either directly or indirectly upon his will, what is there that does depend upon his will, except just the motion of his muscles? If men are not responsible for their predominant passions, dispositions, and desires, then are they under the absolute control of a stern, unbending fate; and no more fit to be held accountable for what they do than automata that move and speak when the master pulls the wire. We can disown responsibility for those states and habits of feeling by which our opinions and conduct are determined, only by disowning the highest attributes of our nature, and casting away the true glory of our being.

Besides, if it be indeed the truth, that men are not responsible for the existence of those states of mind which bias and pervert the judgment, it is a truth which ought to be admitted and acted on in all other matters, as well as in what concerns religion. Admit it, then, in cases like those to which we have referred. Admit that the miser cannot help being what he is, and deserves no censure; that your child is blameless when he quarrels with your judgment; your enemy when he detracts from your well-known merits; and the robber and the murderer when they commit their deeds of darkness. In all these cases, it is in the states of mind previously existing, that the false judgments and the infatuation originate, which impel to the wrong action; and plainly, if there be no responsibility for the first, there can be none whatever for the last. Such is the absurd result to which we come, if we affirm that men are not to be held responsible for their passions, prejudices, and wishes. It makes them blameless, however bad may be their conduct.

It cannot, therefore, save us from being justly held

responsible for our opinions, that the force of evidence is impaired, or neutralized, by our own improper states of mind. Whoever brings to his religious inquiries any other than a humble, candid, willing mind—a mind that honestly desires to know the truth, and is ready to receive it though it should be painful in its nature—will be nearly sure to be lost in error, and must take to himself the blame of all the evil consequences he may suffer.

In the third place, the assertion that men are not to be held responsible for their opinions, assumes yet further, that they have no duty to perform in searching after evidence, and carefully weighing it when found. If no evidence that is satisfactory presents itself, it is imagined there can, of course, be no obligation to believe. If there be a God, and he wishes that mankind should believe in his being and attributes, and in other kindred truths, it belongs to him, it is taken for granted, not merely to *furnish* the evidences of these things, but actually, by his immediate agency, to set them in order before men's minds, and to cause them to be thoroughly known and understood. The whole care of producing belief in this view belongs to God. It is something to be wrought in them, without any toil or thought of theirs, as the sensation of warmth is produced by the solar rays, or by the presence of a fire.

But this view is wholly wrong. No one has any right to take for granted, that if God wishes him to believe particular truths relating to himself, or to his service, he will so set the evidence before his eyes that he cannot choose but see it. It is one of the high distinctions of our being that our intellectual powers are specially adapted to the *pursuit* of truth. The very constitution of our nature thus indicates it as our duty to engage in this pursuit; to apply our minds, actively and earnestly, to the work of investigation, as opportunity is offered. We need no power to search for truth, to explore the sources of proof, and push inquiry to its utmost limits, if our only business is to believe when we cannot help it—when we are actually overpowered with evidence collected for us by other agency than ours and pressed on our passive minds. Yet further, we may ask, How is it, as a matter of experience, in the manifold concerns of life in which our interests are involved? In how many of all the cases in which we form opinions, is it true that we have nothing to do in collecting, arranging, and comparing evidence? How large a part of the care and labour involved in almost every important branch of business consists in doing these very things?

Suppose, for example, you should call upon a farmer, and find him quietly sitting in his house with folded hands in the midst of seed-time; and that, on asking the reason of his conduct, he should coolly tell you that he had no opinion formed as yet as to what kind of grain was best adapted to his soil; but that he was waiting for proof to present itself and settle his uncertainty. Suppose you find a merchant suffering his vessel to lie rotting at the wharf, because not having done anything to ascertain the truth, he has come to no conclusion as to whether or not it will be best to despatch her on a voyage. You would surely think that men who, in such affairs, should take such ground, had either lost their senses, or that they were always fools. But how would the absurdity of such a course be greater than that exhibited by one who, when you ask him of his views in respect to God, religion, and immortality, replies with unconcern that he *has* no settled views about these things, and that he is quietly waiting till evidence shall come to him, and settle finally his doubts? What is there so peculiar in subjects of a religious nature, that the common rules of action are not to be applied to them? That while the merchant, the farmer, and the artizan must set themselves, with diligence and enterprise, to collect and arrange the means of settling their opinions, in their ordinary secular affairs, or be regarded as having lost their sanity; they may go on through life, doing nothing in good earnest to obtain the evidence that should give them certainty as regards their highest interests and duties,—those connected with religion—and incur no such suspicion? There is no reason for any such distinction. The principle in each case, and of course the folly, is the same. In all the great concerns which involve our duty and our welfare,—in those of religion not less, certainly, than others,—we are under imperative obligations to do our utmost to lay hold of, and thoroughly to understand the evidence on which correct opinions must be founded. We must do this, or remain in uncertainty, and quite probably endure the miseries that result from fatal error.

Finally, when it is said that men are not responsible for their opinions, it is obviously assumed that they lack something, either light, or faculties, or opportunity, the giving of which is necessary to render them responsible. If they want nothing which they now have not, to render them responsible, then certainly they *are* responsible. We need not stop to consider how far the responsibility of the degraded and benighted portions of mankind may be modified by their peculiar circumstances. We are speaking, in all this discussion, of civilized men who live surrounded with the means of culture and of knowledge. In all cases, and of course in relation to religious subjects, it is true that two things are necessary to the formation of an intelligent opinion, namely, a proper amount of evidence, and an amount of intellectual power which, if rightly used, is sufficient to understand it. If on any subject, I neither have, nor can have, any fit means of forming an opinion, then all will of course agree that no obligation to form one can possibly exist; and so likewise, incompetency,—the want of understanding to appreciate the force of arguments,—must necessarily forbid the idea of any such obligation. The plea of incompetency is not likely to be urged. If men are competent to think, examine, and decide in regard to other things, they are competent to think, examine, and decide in regard to religious truth. The plea of want of evidence, if urged in relation to the essential truths pertaining to religion, is certainly not valid. It would seem, apart from facts, utterly incredible that no sufficient means of forming an opinion, either one way or the other, should exist, where the matter is so important; and then it is actually found that vast multitudes, and among them minds of the very highest order, do recognise the leading doctrines both of natural and revealed religion, as being sustained by ample proofs—proofs which produce in them the most unwavering conviction. Those too who have examined most thoroughly and with the greatest impartiality and candour, have borne the strongest testimony to the fulness and completeness of the testimony by which these primary doctrines are established; while, on the contrary, those who allege a want of proper evidence, are generally those who have exhibited the least of either diligence or candour in their inquiries. That some, on the other hand, have decidedly rejected the essential truths of religion cannot certainly be urged as proof that no means of forming positive opinions, could be found. They *have* found evidence, they profess, *against* the truth of what are deemed to be the first truths of religion, and have settled their opinions on this basis. There is really no want of evidence, therefore, to those who will carefully and honestly inquire, even by the admission of such as have rejected all religious truths. Those who have received these truths, say they have found evidence sufficient in their favour; those who reject them—that they have found enough on the other side. According to both, there is no lack of the means of forming settled opinions, and nothing to justify a doubtful and unsettled state. Since, therefore, there is nothing wanting in order to make you, or me, or others about us responsible for our opinions, we must be held responsible for these, as truly as for our conduct. We have evidence within our reach; and we may find and use it, if we will. There is nothing in the way of any of us, but an indisposition to apply ourselves, with a serious purpose and an honest mind;

and this surely cannot relieve us from the obligation to find the truth and to embrace and hold it.

It appears then, upon the whole, that the position that men are not responsible for their opinions as regards the main truths of religion, will not stand the test of a fair examination. It is based on assumptions that are false. It overlooks the difference between demonstrative and moral reasoning; the influence of the moral state of the mind upon its judgments; the need there is of care and pains in order to arrive at truth; and the fact that, at least those who are reared in the midst of Christian civilization, have both intellect and evidence enough, if they will rightly use them in the search for truth, to enable them to reach it. All this we have clearly seen.

When, therefore, it is said that "a man's creed does not depend upon himself,"—the reply is, that in the sense in which it is meant to be understood, the assertion is not true. It is plain that those who put in this plea are either self-deceived, or else willing to use this shield against what they know too well to be the shafts of truth. The means of knowledge being given, and the ability to examine and decide, it does depend on every man to determine whether he, as an individual, will know the truth or not. If, for want of due reflection, we ask for demonstration where the nature of the case does not admit it, and refuse to believe without, we must take the blame of doing it. If we suffer our personal feelings and desires to warp and blind us, when we ought to be single minded, we must take the blame of doing it. If we are too indifferent or too heedless to examine the proofs that actually exist and may be found by proper effort, we must take the blame of doing it. If we wait for something to be done for us, or something to be given us, to fill up the measure of our responsibility, when nothing really is wanting, we must take the blame of doing it. It would be just as near the truth to say that a man's actions do not depend upon himself, as to affirm this of his opinions in respect to the more elementary religious truths.

"But who can say"—it is asked—"I *will* believe this, that, or the other?" Observe the sophistry involved in this inquiry—as though there could be no way of doing voluntarily, and in the use of our own powers, what cannot be done by a simple act of will! Suppose it were pressed on me as a duty to visit, for some good purpose, a distant place, and that I should answer, "Who can say I *will* be in this, that, or the other place"—as if I supposed it meant that I should put myself there at once by simply willing it. You would justly pronounce it a mere quibble; for no one would think of asking me to do any such thing as that. I cannot, indeed, transport myself to a distant place by an effort of my will; but I *can* use my powers and means to go, if I am so disposed. I cannot will myself directly into the belief of any truth; but I can rightly use my powers and means to come to a clear conviction of it. This makes me just as much responsible for my belief, as though I could *will belief*, as directly as I will to lift my arm. So common sense does certainly decide.

It is altogether in vain, then, that we endeavour to comfort ourselves in a state of doubt or error, with the persuasion that we are not responsible for our opinions. We *are* responsible! In matters of such moment as religion; on questions of such magnitude as those relating to the existence and attributes of God, the immortality of the soul, and the reality of revelation; to the great rules of human duty, the way of being permanently happy, and the certainty of future retribution; there *must* be means of arriving at fixed conclusions—we cannot think it otherwise without doing violence to our own reason and the instincts of our own souls—and it must be a high abuse of our rational endowments, to neglect or to misuse these means.

If any of you say that you have not hitherto been able, and are not able now, to reach results that satisfy you, then you are bound to show beyond all doubt that the fault is not in you—that you have approached religious subjects as you ought, and without prejudice or bias, have done your utmost to come to fixed and just conclusions. Can you say this, O doubter, if there be one such in this assembly? Do you not rather feel in the depths of your secret soul, on the bare proposing of the question, that you have been most culpably neglectful and careless in the matter? Within yourself, then, lies the difficulty. Until with a truly childlike, open, earnest mind, you have *tasked your highest powers and failed*, you cannot rid yourself of the vast responsibility of being firmly fixed in right religious opinions. God, who has given you such power of thought, such inward light of reason, and such outward means of knowledge—who every day and hour is speaking to you, through all the beauty, and wisdom, and grandeur of the universe; in the stupendous march of his eternal Providence; in the monitions of conscience, and the deep instinctive yearning of your immortal nature; and, as the wisest and the best of all mankind believe, in a positive revelation, by which a glorious stream of light from out the ineffable splendours of his throne, has fallen on your way, and a voice of infinite sweetness from the bosom of his love has spoken to your soul—this God, who knows you, and cares for you, and will sit at last to judge your conduct, according to all that he has done to elevate and bless you—*must* hold you, *does* hold you, *will* hold you in the day of his great award of retribution, responsible for your belief, or unbelief, in relation to his being and your duty as his creature. He bids you search for wisdom as for rubies, and promises divine illumination to all who humbly ask it. It is for *you* then to determine, as you will answer for yourself to Him, whether you will know and love the truth and be the children of the light.

—"Faith is the subtle chain
That binds us to the Infinite; the voice
Of a deep life within that will remain
Until we crowd it thence!"

IV.

The Practical Value of Opinions.

PROV. xxiii. 23: *Buy the truth and sell it not.*

IT is a saying of our blessed Lord himself, that the children of this world are wise in their generation. By this he meant that, in the common affairs of life, they exhibit shrewdness and discernment in consulting their own interests. If there be anything which they regard as valuable and believe to be within their reach, they spare no pains or effort in order to obtain it; and when once they have satisfied themselves that any particular possession will be of permanent advantage, they are ready to buy it at any price, and when bought, they steadily refuse to part with it again. This is sound worldly wisdom; sound wisdom, that is, in regard to worldly things.

Precisely the same course the wisest of men enjoins in relation to the acquiring and the retaining of the truth—of all truth, but more especially that which directly pertains to the highest and most enduring welfare of mankind. Truth of this sort is of inestimable value. It is a pearl of great price; more precious than rubies; and he is the happiest of men who buys, never to sell it again, although he part with all he has to make the purchase. This, on the bare statement, would seem to be too obvious to be insisted on in the way of argument. One would as soon expect to hear the worth of gold and diamonds disputed, as to hear any question raised as to the worth of religious truth.

But there is hardly anything so plain in respect to human duty, that a wrong state of moral feeling may not cause it to be doubted, or even to be denied; and strange as it may seem, it is an everyday occurrence to hear the value of truth itself disputed. It is common to hear those who are drifting about in loose uncertainty, gravely advance the sentiment that religious opinions, convictions, as to what is true and real in matters of religion, are of but very little consequence; and having in the last discourse shown the futility of the plea that men are not responsible for their opinions, we will now examine the kindred allegation that opinions are of no practical importance. It is usually stated thus: "It is no matter what a man believes, if his life is only right." The assertion sounds as familiar, and even trite, as though it were one of the plainest imaginable truths; and yet it will appear on examination to be one of the most glaring and self-evident of falsehoods. It will be seen to be very much as if it should be said, "It is no matter whether a man have eyes or not, provided only that he can see!" To act right without knowledge is hardly less a practicable thing, than to see without the proper organs.

For consider what is necessary to be done in order to prove the position true that it is no matter what a man believes on religious subjects if his life be right. It must be shown either, first, that there *are* no certain truths pertaining to religion; or else, secondly, that these truths have no necessary connection with the conduct of men; or else, thirdly, that the consequences of their conduct, whether right or wrong, will be the same.

We ask, then, in the first place, how it can be shown that there are, in religion, no fixed, unchangeable facts; that there is no nature and constitution of things which exists as positive reality? In physical science—the science of material nature—it is acknowledged that there are facts, truths, laws; and is it to be believed, is it in any way capable of proof, that in the universe of mind and the sphere of moral science, there are no such things—no realities, or at least none that can be known? Pray, let us have the proof, you who take this remarkable position. It will be very singular indeed, should you be able to make out, that while there are indisputable certainties in all other departments of our knowledge, there are none in that which includes the spiritual nature and relations of our being, and our best and highest, because our eternal, interests. Let us look at the matter a little in detail, in order that what we mean may be clearly understood.

We will draw an illustration from commerce. You have great interests, we will suppose, involved in this. You freight your ships for distant places and dispatch them, calculating, under certain conditions, on such and such results. In this affair there are, you very well know, certain fixed and unalterable facts, or truths—things which can be known definitely and fully. As to the sea, for example, it is a fact that it has a determinate shape and size; that it has its ebb and flow of tides; that it has its Gulf Stream, and other well-known currents;

that rocks and shoals are hidden in its bosom; and that its condition is variously affected by the action of storm and wind. As to the winds themselves it is a fact that in some regions they are variable, in others constant in their direction; that at some seasons and in some places, they are sure to be tempestuous, and in others certain to be calm; that at one time the land breeze may be counted on, and at another the opposite; and lastly, that the rise or fall of the barometer betoken particular changes of the weather. As to the ship, in any given case, she is known to have a certain capacity, or to be of a certain burthen; her sails and rigging have a certain relation to her size; she requires, with a given freight, a certain depth of water; with a certain amount of pressure she will attain a particular speed; and a certain number of hands are required to man her. She carries a chart; it is the result of careful and accurate surveys. She has a compass; it obeys a well-known law with certain slight variations that have been ascertained and noted. And so we might go on.

Let it be observed, then, that in so ordinary a matter as the sending of a ship to a foreign port, all these, and many other things, are recognised as necessarily existing facts. They are involved in the very nature of the transaction. They are the truths pertaining to the case; and should any one assert to you that in this commercial enterprise there were no facts or truths involved, you would simply think him wanting in common sense.

But here are multitudes of intelligent creatures who have entered on the great arena of existence. They must think, they must feel, they must act, they must permanently enjoy or suffer. They have a conscious capacity for religious responsibilities; a conscience which recognises the difference between right and wrong, and feels the obligation of the former; and a sense of dependence and of restlessness within the heart, which seems to be the expression of constitutional religious wants. As these beings could not have given themselves existence, they acknowledge a Creator. As they are frail and in many respects helpless, they naturally conceive themselves to be connected with him as objects of his care and providence. It seems a reasonable thought that they must owe him some important duties, that he must have had some object in giving them existence, and must, of course, have some choice as to what they shall be and do. It is difficult for them not to think that it must make some difference in their feelings and condition, whether they act according to his design, or in opposition to it, and whether their religious cravings are satisfied or not. Therefore it would appear as though there are, of necessity, implied in the very existence and relations of these creatures certain definite and most essential facts, certain things which are true and real, and may be ascertained and known to be so.

But you will have it that there are no realities in matters of religion; no facts, that is, which exist in the nature of things and which may be either revealed or laid open to observation. Then clearly it belongs to you to show, to prove beyond dispute and against the reason, and consciousness, and common sense of men, that there is no Creator, that man is not a dependent creature, that he has no spiritual nature, that his moral instincts and judgments are all alike illusive, that he has no moral obligations of any sort whatever, and that there is no difference between right and wrong. These appear to be the primary facts of religion just as the existence of the sun and planets, with their mutual relations and the law of gravitation, are the primary facts of astronomy. Disprove the existence of the sun, and planets, and gravitation, and astronomical science will be effectually demolished. Disprove the being of God and of the soul, their relations to each other, and the essential distinction between moral good and evil, and you will as effectually demolish all religion. You will hardly undertake to do so much so this. Nothing but sheer atheism, and that but very rarely, has attempted to go so far.

It is plain that the very notion of religion supposes certain things to be true, as matters of fact and as being necessarily recognised as true and real, unless religion itself be abjured as a chimera. Man has a certain moral nature, he has certain moral relations, these give rise to certain duties, and his actions, considered as right or wrong, are connected with certain fixed results. These facts, as existing in the nature of things, are not changed by our misapprehensions and wrong beliefs about them when we wander into error. They are unalterable realities. There are such realities in the moral world not less than in the natural.

We come, then, to the other side of the alternative. We ask, in the second place, how it can be shown that the actually existing facts, the real truths in regard to the religious interests and obligations of mankind, have no necessary connection with their moral conduct? This is what is taken for granted in the plea for unsettled, or wrong opinions, which we are now considering. When it is said that it is no matter what a man believes, if his life be only right, it is said, in effect, that a man's belief has no determining influence on his conduct; that his opinions, his views of truth, are one affair, and his actions quite another; for if opinions do influence the conduct, do even, as the rule at least, determine it, then it is not and cannot be true that it is immaterial what they are.

Let us go back to our commercial illustration. Let us see how it would answer to assume in the supposed affair of dispatching a vessel to a foreign port, that it is no matter what a man believes. Let us see whether there is not of necessity an inseparable connection between the opinions of the master of the vessel and his conduct—whether his views of facts *can* be radically wrong, and yet his course of conduct be all right. How is it, then? Your captain has a fixed belief as to the distance he has to run, as to the strength and direction of the currents, as to the position of banks and ledges, as to the laws which regulate the wind and weather, as to the capacities of his ship and the supplies which he requires, as to the correctness of his chart and the accuracy of his compass. He has certain established opinions or convictions in respect to all these and many similar things. What think you, then—have his opinions, or have they not, an influence on his conduct? Do they, or do they not, affect his mode of planning and executing the voyage to be performed? Apply the adage—It is no matter what he believes, if his conduct be but right! Ah, yes! but let him believe the opposite of what is actually true. Let him honestly believe that his proper course is east when really his port lies west; let him entertain the opinion that the prevailing currents are setting southward, when in fact they are setting to the north; let him persuade himself that his ship is twice as strong as she is in truth, and that she draws but half the water that she actually does; let him have confidence in an inaccurate chart, and adopt too little or too much as the variation of the needle. With these views, which are directly contrary to the facts, *will* his conduct—*can* his conduct by any possibility be the same as if he believed in accordance with the facts? Will not his opinions determine his conduct in the case, and of necessity make it wrong? Can any one suppose, without a sense of the absurdity of such a supposition, that his actions can be right as regards his voyage, while his opinions, his judgment as to essential facts, are altogether wrong.

But in matters of religion, it may be said, the case is different. Pray be so kind as to tell us how, if you are able. The soul is certainly a thing which has a nature and qualities of its own, as truly as a ship. It is just as truly fitted for some purposes, and unfitted for others, by its very constitution. It is made capable of finding happiness in certain things, and not in others. In a certain course of action its faculties expand; it rises in the scale of being, and seems to exist for a noble end; in an opposite course it degenerates and grovels, and appears to live for no important purpose. It is competent to know God and to love and obey him; and when it does this it has peace within itself. When it fails to do this, it feels inwardly dissatisfied and restless; and generally, in the doing of what is right it has a sense of pleasure, and in the doing of what is wrong a consciousness of pain. These are existing facts in respect to the human soul, considered as having a moral nature and relations. Take any individual man, these facts are true of him; and we will suppose that he believes them fully. He believes that he has a responsible soul; that it must find its happiness in a certain way, or not at all; that right and wrong are immutably distinct, the one connected necessarily with pleasure, and the other as necessarily with pain; that God as his Creator, and as the infinitely Wise and Good, is entitled to his love and his obedience, and will reward or punish him, according as he renders these, or not. Is it conceivable that the belief of these should have no influence on his conduct? Believing them with firm conviction, will his course of living be just the same, as if he did not believe them? Is it just the same, so far as his actions are concerned, whether he believes that he has an immortal nature, or believes that he has none? whether he thinks that the love and pursuit of what is pure and good will make him happy, or of what is corrupt and evil? whether he concludes that he is accountable to God and a subject of reward or punishment, or that he has no responsibility at all? whether he thinks that virtue and vice are moral opposites, or that there is nothing to choose between them? This is what you say, however unconsciously, when you assert that it is no matter what a man believes, if his life be only right. You say that his opinions have *no relation* to his life. You say that in order to act according to the nature of his soul, it is no matter whether he believes that he has a soul! That in order to do right it is no matter whether he believes that there is any such thing as right! That in order to meet his responsibilities to God, it is no matter whether he believes that he is responsible at all, or even whether there be a God or not! A man's opinions and his life are wholly independent of each other. His opinions may be all wrong, all contrary to the actual facts, and his course of action none the less all right!

What, then, we would like to be informed, determines a man's course of action; what leads him to act as he does act, if his views of things do not? A thoughtful child can see that it is a man's views of things, his opinions, what he believes, that mainly determines his character and conduct, and make his course of life just what it is. When appetite and inclination draw men away to evil, they do this mainly through their perverting influence on the judgment persuading them to accept the false as true —to believe wrong and then act wrong. To talk of a man's believing wrong, as to essential truths or facts, and at the same time acting right, is to talk absurdly. It is of the highest moment that a man's belief accord with the reality of things, because unless it does, he cannot act according to the reality of things; his life cannot be right. It may possibly be right in its outward seeming, but in its real spirit and aims, it will be wrong.

But since it cannot be denied, with any show of reason,

that a man's actions depend essentially on his opinions, and will be mainly determined by them, the third alternative may be adopted. It may be said, it has been often said, that if one only *thinks* that he is acting right, it will make no difference in the end, the result to him will be just the same, whether he really acts right or not. If a man believe wrong, and act wrong in the whole moral ordering of his life, so he do this but sincerely, no serious harm will follow. In some way or other it will come out about as well as if he had believed and done precisely what he ought.

But what is this, when you examine it, but the palpably false assertion that actions have no natural and necessary consequences? Actions are causes, whose effects follow with the certainty of inexorable law, according to the established moral order of the universe. It is a part of the nature of things, that believing right and acting right, each human being will certainly reap the rewards of his well doing; but that believing wrong and acting wrong, each must inevitably encounter the consequences of his error. It is this that gives its highest importance to a man's religious belief. As that determines his character and conduct, so it must finally determine his destiny of happiness or woe.

We have only to try the notion that the consequences of right and wrong action may be in the end the same, in any concern of common life to see how absurd it is. Refer again, if you please, to commerce. If ever so sincerely, your captain believes that Cuba lies in the Mediterranean sea or in the Indian Ocean, will he therefore find it there?

If he sincerely thinks that there are five fathoms of water on a bar, when in fact there is but one, will that prevent the striking of his vessel? Or if it is his opinion that his cable is sound and strong when really it is rotten, will that prevent him, when the tempest rages, from being swept from his moorings and dashed a wreck upon the rocks? If he does not regard the facts as they actually exist, there is nothing that can prevent the consequences of his ignorance. The case is in no wise different in the matter of religion. In this, as in other things, facts are facts whatever we may think about them. If sin by the nature of things does lead to misery, and a man ever so sincerely believes that it leads to happiness, it will lead to misery still. If a man build his house—the edifice of his immortal hopes—on the shifting sand, persuading himself that he builds on solid rock, it will none the less for his sincerity in error, fall with a terrible destruction, when the rain descends, and the winds blow, and the floods come. If a man convince himself that he can live without God and be happy, while it is true that God alone can meet his spiritual wants, he will yet be sure to feel at last the anguish of an empty and wretched heart. Such is the nature of things, and such it will be, whatever one believes. Is it, then, no matter what a man believes? Is it just as safe and just as well at last, to be in error as to understand the truth—to act against the laws of our own nature and of the moral universe, as to act in accordance with them? If so, the more complete the blindness and delusion in which men sink and keep themselves the better; for they escape by this means all anxiety about the truth, and in the end come off as well. A conclusion so abhorrent to reason and right thinking, who can be willing to admit?

The result, then, to which we are brought is this: that it is not to be expected that the conduct, the lives of men, will be materially better than their opinions. Of course, in all that we have said, we have intended to refer, not to the opinions men profess, but to the actual living convictions of their minds. These, we have seen, do stand in direct and determining relation to their actions; and their actions to certain natural and necessary consequences, so that it may be said, with little qualification, that a man's religious opinions, his real views of religious truth, do in fact decide his character and fix his destiny, as a moral and accountable being; that as these are true or false, the man, in any case, will be good or bad in his moral conduct, and happy or miserable in his ultimate condition.

It is plainly, therefore, an imperative duty to set a high value upon truth in our religious thinking. Of what vast importance it is seen to be, that your religious opinions should not only be firmly fixed, but that they should also be *right* opinions!—As it is indispensable to the welfare of the body that you have right opinions as to what is wholesome food and what is poison, what exercise and regimen are salutary and what sure to prove pernicious, even so, you perceive, it is in relation to the soul. Acting on the false and dangerous maxim that it is no matter what a man believes, you are every moment liable to embrace such errors as will, by their practical influence and effects, poison the fountains of your immortal happiness and prostrate the health and vigour of your immortal powers. If on the great voyage of existence you trust a lying chart, a deceitful compass and a treacherous pilot, nothing can save you from the woes of fatal wreck. Wrong ways lead infallibly to ruin, whatever they may think that travel in them. Right ways lead infallibly to safety, whatever they may think that turn their backs upon them. Be sure, my fellow-mortal,—since your duty and your personal well-being alike demand it of you,—be sure that in forming your religious opinions you dig deep and build on the rock of eternal truth.

But perhaps the thought, or at least the feeling, arises in your mind, that it is too much trouble to ascertain the truth. You have done nothing hitherto, in serious earnest, towards learning what it is, because there is so much to be done. Strange apathy and inconsistency, where so much is at stake! The artizan cannot rest till he learns all the important facts about his art. The merchant never faints in his efforts to find out all the principles and laws of trade. The farmer perseveres till he has informed himself on all important points about his farm. But in respect to God and immortality—to the nature, relations, and destiny of the ever-living soul within you, *you* are content to be in ignorance, and to think nothing on the subject, or only in the way of idle speculation! In this way some of you may have lived for many years. God has given you ample means, instructions, books, and wise religious counsellors, yet here you are, in the same condition still, all uncertainty and doubt, and, strangest of the whole, quite unconcerned about your state!

But, *mtie* the meanwhile—I beg you to consider it—has not been standing still. It has been silently sweeping on with a mighty current towards the shadows of the unseen world, and bearing you forward on its bosom. Yet a little longer, and even for you who are in the strength of your early years, eternity will open with the expanse of its everlasting ages. It will find you as you are, the children of darkness and not of light, unless you bestir yourselves right soon; and oh! rely upon it, you will find at last, that there are real facts pertaining to your soul, and to its duties and destinies for ever, which it was of infinite importance for you to have known betimes. You will see clearly then that the difference between religious truth and error, was as wide as that between eternal life and death—between heaven itself and hell. See to it, I pray you, that you have not then to look back, with the anguish of a bitter self-reproach, on neglected opportunities, and an unprofitable and wasted life.

Ah—the truth!—the truth in relation to ourselves, our duty, our happiness, as the rational creatures of God—it is indeed the richest of all gems! Buy it, you who are young—buy it all of you, at any price, and never let it go. Error will sooner or later perish; and they who trust in it will perish with it. But TRUTH shall change and pass away, only when God himself shall die!

V.

Belief in the Being of God.

Ps. xiv. 1: *The fool hath said in his heart, There is no God.*

A BELIEF in God, as a self-existent, intelligent, and infinitely perfect Being, is the basis of all religion. Law, supposes a lawgiver; accountability, a governor and judge; and worship, a real object of affection and devotion. If there were no God, there would be, to the human race, no right and wrong, no feeling of moral obligation, no virtue, no vice, no piety; nothing to constitute a moral nature, or to call forth moral action. The sole impulses which could operate to move men, on such a supposition, would be instinct, and expediency considered in reference to self-interest.

It is not, however, enough, that we admit the divine existence. It is highly desirable, not only to entertain a firm conviction that God exists, but also clearly to understand, if possible, in what manner, or through what means, we come by this conviction. On this point there has been much discussion, and widely different views, among the philosophers and thinking men fo every age. Some have maintained the idea of God to be innate; as Cicero for example, who says: * *Omnibus enim innatum*

* De Natura Deorum, b. ii., cap. xii.

est, et in animo quasi insculptum—that it is inborn in all men, and as it were engraven on the mind. Others have asserted the divine existence to be an intuition—an immediate perception of the reason, independently of any suggestion, argument, or evidence. By others again, it has been attempted to establish it by the rigid steps of mathematical demonstration. Nearly all agree that the constitution and the course of nature suggest an infinite intelligence; and it has also been insisted, more especially by Kant and those who have followed him, that the moral nature of man—his conscience and sense of moral obligation—affords conclusive proof of the being and moral government of God.

That a belief of the divine existence is innate, in the proper sense, the soundest philosophy forbids us to believe. That the truth that there is a God is strictly and purely an intuition, does not by any means appear. It is likewise pretty generally conceded that the proposition does not fall within the province of mathematical reasoning, and that the so-called demonstrations of it have in fact been failures. We believe the true statement of the matter to be this: That the human mind is *constitutionally fitted* to know God,—so that the notion of him, and a persuasion of his existence, *necessarily arise* within the soul whenever the faculties are in any good degree developed; and that in its own moral consciousness, and in a great variety of facts and phenomena external to itself, it finds, on reflection, proofs that he does exist,—proofs of a moral nature, yet sufficient to establish the fact as an absolute certainty, in the view of the understanding.

Such being the facts in relation to this great question. it is plain that the force of the evidence of the divine existence does not depend on any single proof or mode of argument considered by itself, but, as in other cases of moral or probable reasoning, on the entire impression which all proofs that can be gathered from all sources, are adapted to produce when taken in combination. Our proper method is, to avail ourselves of every fact and every circumstance which has the least significance; to seize on the slightest intimations of a Deity, as well as on the most palpable and convincing attestations of his being; and in this way to accumulate our evidence till it rises before us like one vast mountain, commanding in its aspect, and for ever immovable on its firm foundations.

In accordance with this view, it is proposed in this discourse to call your attention to certain generally admitted facts, which cannot but have great weight, if seriously and candidly considered, as they bear, especially when taken together, on the question of the divine existence.

First of all, it is a well-known fact, that the idea of God and of spiritual existence is, and has always been, nearly or quite universal among mankind.

Among all nations which have attained to any good degree of civilization, the idea of God, or of gods, one of whom was above the rest, has been perfectly familiar. The most barbarous and degraded even, who in some instances have seemed, on a slight acquaintance with them, to have no such conception, have been found, on further examination, to entertain it. Along with the idea of God has been found also that of a spiritual world, and of spiritual existence and agency, in a variety of forms. Hence the mythologies, some of them highly poetical and beautiful, which grew up under the polished culture of the Greeks and Romans, and the more grotesque and fanciful systems of Oriental nations. It is, doubtless, true that among the less enlightened portions of mankind the notion of God has been extremely gross and every way defective. Forasmuch as they have not liked to retain God in their knowledge, they have become vain in their imaginations, and their foolish hearts have been darkened. But of this we have no occasion now to speak. It is the fact that this idea, in any degree of development whatever, should so universally prevail that claims our present notice, and requires an explanation. How shall it be accounted for in a way to satisfy the thoughtful mind? Whence comes it that the whole human race appear to be under a kind of constitutional necessity of forming and entertaining an idea to which there exists no object—no reality—to correspond? If there is a God, the infinite and intelligent Creator of all things, it is but natural, in the view of enlightened reason, that man should be so made, and his circumstances so arranged, that some notion of the Great Author and Preserver of his being should necessarily arise within his soul. But say that there is no God, and it appears wholly unaccountable—a phenomenon without a cause—that such a conception, more or less imperfect as the case may be, should be found to spring up, as if by a moral instinct, in every human bosom.

It is equally a matter of common observation that the more thoughtful, and especially the more virtuous men are, the more, as the general rule, they are disposed to *cherish* the idea of a supreme Being.

It will be admitted that the more the mind is addicted to serious reflection and inquiry after truth, and the more pure and virtuous it is in its tastes and dispositions, the nearer it approaches to its true normal state—that is, to the state of right and healthful action to which it is constitutionally adapted. Or to put the same thing differently, everybody will allow that just in proportion as men are intelligent and good they are likely to be free from perverting influences, and clearly to perceive truth as it actually is. It would not seem a strange thing that mind in an abnormal condition, disordered through ignorance and vice, should be led to entertain erroneous and unfounded notions; but if that which appears to be the truth to mind in its highest and best condition, and which is found universally to become the more certain to it, the more and the better it investigates, may after all be only an illusion, then there can be no such thing as positive truth, nothing of real unquestionable knowledge within the reach of man.

When, therefore, we observe that to serious thinkers and the lovers of true virtue, in all ages and among all nations, the idea of God has been not only a familiar, but a favourite idea—that, generally, the conviction of the existence of an infinitely perfect Being has been clear and strong in proportion as the intelligence has been superior and the virtue unequivocal, we are plainly in this dilemma—that we must deny the certainty of human knowledge altogether, or else we must believe that there is substantial evidence that such a being does actually exist. Either we are so constituted that in the best use of our highest faculties we are naturally led to believe and love a falsehood, or else there is, in the existence of a supreme Being, a personal God, an objective reality, corresponding to the idea which the enlightened mind is disposed to entertain, and to the belief in which it feels itself the more constrained to rest, the more elevated and pure are its affections, and the more liberal and profound its knowledge.

It is also a fact not to be disputed, that a belief in the existence of a God has always been found exceedingly difficult to be eradicated.

Notwithstanding that, as already noticed, the notion of a supreme Being appears to arise naturally in the minds of all men who have any intellectual culture, there have still been professed atheists in every age. But in relation to these there are two things to be particularly observed. The first is, that it has always been apparent that they established themselves in the disbelief of the divine existence, only after great, and usually long-continued, striving against an inward conviction of the probability, at least, of the being of a God. They have shown how strong was the tendency of their minds towards theism, by their eagerness to find out arguments against it, and by their readiness to lay hold of any that could be made to seem available, even though they were really sophistical and weak. They have, in general, very obviously found it difficult to keep their minds at rest in a state of disbelief to such a degree as to relieve them from the constant necessity of labouring to fortify themselves in their position.

The other thing deserving notice in respect to those professing atheism is, that when they had seemed to be confirmed in the rejection of the doctrine of a God, it has often happened that the influence of some comparatively trifling circumstance or argument has been sufficient to neutralize entirely their unbelief almost in a single moment; and the conviction that there must be, or certainly that there may be a deity after all, has come back upon their minds with overwhelming power. When they had pronounced the idea of God a mere chimera, and had imagined themselves for ever emancipated from the superstition of admitting it, they have found that there still seemed to be a something, in the deep recesses of the soul, that would sometimes whisper the unwelcome thought with a startling distinctness, and make it seem, at least for the time, an unquestionable reality. I once found, in a meeting for religious inquiry, an intelligent young man whom I had never seen before. He seemed to feel intensely. Seating myself by his side, I asked in what state of mind he was. "O sir," said he, "I do not know myself. I was an atheist a little while ago, or thought I was, but now it has all gone from me. I feel—I know—now that there is a God!" Many such instances occur—sometimes under the influence of revivals of religion, sometimes in the season of affliction, in the moment of danger, or in the hour of death. They are impressive illustrations of the difficulty with which a belief in the divine existence can be totally eradicated, when once developed in the mind. They make it clear that the most confirmed atheist can never be quite sure that he will not find his unbelief forsaking him, just when he will want it most, and the unwelcome conviction which he had thought for ever banished returning on him with overwhelming force.

How, then, shall we account for this? Some good reason certainly there must be, for this great difficulty, universally experienced, in attempting to rid the mind in which the idea of God has been developed of a conviction of his existence. The phenomenon cannot be accidental; it exhibits too much of the constancy of established law. To what can we refer it but to a constitutional adaptation of the mind to receive the truth that there is a God, taken in connection with the objective certainty of the truth itself. This plainly is the only satisfactory solution. There is no other which is even plausible.

We may further add, in the fourth place, that the atheistical hypothesis, or, in other words, the supposition that no God exists, when fully and distinctly placed before the mind, is abhorrent to the moral feelings of the soul.

It is obvious that men may speak, and often do speak, of the non-existence of a Deity without any distinct notion of what this really involves; and it is because they speak inconsiderately and ignorantly that they are not conscious of any strong repugnance to the admission of the thought. Or if, in the case of those who have utterly abandoned themselves to evil, and who, in the depth of their depravity, appear to wish there were no God, the hypothesis of atheism, when deliberately considered, does not awaken feelings of abhorrence; it is only because the non-existence of God is regarded as a less dreadful evil than the suffering of eternal punishment. If there were no God, it would by no means follow either that the wicked would cease to be at death, or that if they should continue to exist they would be happy. But while they flatter themselves that such would be the consequence, this hope of impunity may in a measure reconcile them to the idea of a universe without a Deity.

With some such partial, and perhaps only apparent exceptions, it is certainly true, that the moral sentiments of the human soul do so earnestly demand a God, that the serious supposition that none exists, is one from which the heart shrinks, as dark and horrible in the last degree.

A German writer, the celebrated Jean Paul Richter, illustrates this revulsion of the moral instincts of the soul from atheism, in a passage of such surpassing impressiveness and power, that I am tempted to quote it, notwithstanding the strangeness of the style in which it is conceived and executed. It takes the form of a dream, and has a wildness which only a German imagination could have imparted to the treatment of such a subject; but the entire impression which it makes is truthful and profound. It is as follows:—

"I was reclining one summer evening on the summit of a hill, and falling asleep there, I dreamed that I awoke in the middle of the night in a church-yard. The clock struck eleven. The tombs were all half open, and the iron gates of the church moved by an invisible hand, opened and shut again with a great noise. I saw shadows flitting along the walls, which were not cast by any bodily substance. Other livid spectres rose in the air, and children alone still reposed in their coffins. There was a greyish, heavy stifling cloud in the sky, which was strained and compressed into long folds by a gigantic phantom. Above me I heard the distant fall of avalanches, and under my feet the first commotion of a mighty earthquake. The church shook, and the air was agitated by piercing and discordant sounds.

"The pale lightning cast a mournful light. I felt myself impelled by terror to seek shelter in the temple. Two splendid basilisks were placed before its formidable gates.

"I advanced amid the crowd of unknown shades on whom the seal of ancient ages was imprinted. They all pressed around the despoiled altar; and their breasts only breathed and were agitated with violence. One corpse alone which had been lately buried in the church reposed on its winding sheet; there was yet no motion in its breast, and a pleasing dream gave a smile to its countenance; but at the approach of a living being it awoke, ceased to smile, and opened its heavy eyelids with a painful effort. The socket of the eye was empty, and where the heart had been there was only a deep wound. It raised its hands and joined them to pray; but the arms lengthened, were detached from the body, and the clasped hands fell to the earth.

"In the vaulted ceiling of the church was placed the dial of eternity. No figures or index were there, but a black hand went slowly round, and the dead endeavoured to read on it the lapse of time.

"From the high places there then descended on the altar a figure beaming with light, noble, elevated, but who bore the impression of never-ending sorrow. The dead cried out, 'O Christ! is there then no God?' He replied, 'There is none.' All the spectres then began to tremble violently, and Christ continued thus, 'I have traversed worlds, I have raised myself above their suns, and there, also, there is no God! I have descended to the lowest limits of the universe; I looked into the abyss, and I cried, O Father, where art thou?' Yet I heard nothing but the rain that fell drop by drop into the abyss, and the everlasting and ungovernable tempest alone answered me. Then raising my regards to the vault of heaven, I saw only an empty orbit, dark and bottomless. Eternity reposed on chaos, and in gnawing it, slowly also devoured itself. Redouble, then, your piercing and bitter complaints. May shrill cries disperse your spirits, for all hope is over.

"The spectres of despair vanished, like the white vapour condensed by the frost. The church was soon deserted. But all at once—terrific sight—the dead children who were now awakened in their turn in the church-yard, ran and prostrated themselves before the majestic figure which was on the altar, saying to him, 'Jesus, have we no Father?' And he replied with a torrent of tears, 'We are all orphans! Neither I nor you have any Father!' At these words, the temple and the children were swallowed up, and all the edifice of the world sunk before me into the immensity of space."

Appalling as this picture is, of the anguish and despair which would overwhelm the spirits of men were it authoritatively announced to them that the idea of God was a chimera, that the universe was without a head, and all beings without a Father—it is yet a picture by no means overdrawn. Let any one who is disposed to doubt on this point, make a deliberate and fair appeal to his own consciousness, and he will find how abhorrent to his whole moral nature is the conception of a universe without a Deity; the blind, dark, dismal reign of forces eternally conflicting, without unity and without intelligence, instead of the dominion of wisdom and of love embodied in a personal and infinitely perfect God. Why in all nature does the seed sprout upward, plant it as you will? Because, by an inward law, it is determined to seek the genial influence of the sun. Even so the human soul has deep within itself a something—call it a yearning, or an instinct, or whatever else you choose—a sense of want profound and uneradicable—which, until it be utterly destroyed by sin, so causes it to feel the need of God, that even while it does not truly love him, it cannot endure the thought of his non-existence.

What, then, shall be said by way of accounting for so remarkable a fact? Is there more than one solution which will at all commend itself to any serious, thinking mind? Does it not seem a gross absurdity to entertain the thought, that the rational soul of man is constitutionally disposed to search after, and to demand as an absolute necessity in order to its happiness, a living, personal Deity, if no such being really exists? Can it be possibly conceived that atheism should be so abhorrent to the best feelings of the heart in man, so intolerable to think of, if the atheistical hypothesis be not a falsehood and an absurdity?

We refer, in the fifth place, to yet another fact which is of great significance. It is clearly proved by the experience of all ages, that a belief in the existence of one supreme and perfect God is in a high degree elevating and happy in the influence which it exerts on the mind and heart of man; while the views of atheism have tended only to demoralization and debasement.

It, doubtless, has sometimes been true that individuals have been found who have professed atheism, and yet have not materially departed outwardly from the observances of virtue. But these have been chiefly such as have been born and educated where the institutions, and the whole spirit of society, were determined by a very general belief in the divine existence; and to this it has been owing, that the appropriate effects of their unbelief have not appeared. So obvious have been the pernicious tendencies of atheism, even where the prevalent ideas of God were exceedingly erroneous, that philosophers and statesmen who studied to promote the well-being of society, have regarded the popular belief of polytheism, bringing along with it all the evils of idolatry, as safer far, and greatly less corrupting, than the atheistical denial of any power superior to man and nature. They dared not disturb the popular faith in divine existence and agency, corrupted and imperfect as it was, and even seemed to coun tenance it, although they had themselves attained to better views, because they saw that under the reign of universal atheism all the virtues that adorn humanity, and even society itself would perish.

On the other hand, the fact lies on the very face of

human history, that a settled belief in the being of a God, and of the truths which are obviously deducible from this, is not only favourable in its influence on human character and happiness, but favourable in a very high degree. The existence of a Deity admitted, the doctrines of a Providence, of human responsibility, and of ultimate retribution, logically follow, and are, of course, admitted likewise; and all these truths taken together, must, from the nature of the case, tend powerfully to develop the feeling of moral obligation in the soul, and to put restraint on all its propensities to evil. Such have been everywhere their manifest effects. If it is true, and it must certainly be admitted to be true, that in communities and states in which there has been a prevalent acknowledgment of the divine existence, there have been but too many exhibitions of popular depravity, it will also be found on inquiry to be true that when corruption of manners has most obtained, faith in a Deity has been least real; and on the contrary, it will appear that when faith in God has been most intelligent, most vital and prevailing, the evil impulses of men have been most restrained, and the flowers and the fruits of virtue have most richly bloomed and ripened throughout all the walks of life. Refer, for example, if you please, to Jewish history. There were periods in which their belief in the one true God was general, deep, and earnest. Those were the bright and glorious periods of their national existence. There were days in which they lost the freshness and the vigour of their faith in the great Jehovah, and even lapsed into actual idolatry; and those were the days in which both public and private virtue disappeared, and there was seen everywhere the sad and abhorrent picture of individual baseness, and of social rottenness and misery; and even at the worst, their moral condition was far better than that of the nations immediately around them, among whom there was no faith in the one true God at all. It is impossible to read the glowing passages of David and Isaiah, in which they delineate with such surpassing power and beauty the character and attributes of the Most High, without believing that the grand idea of divine perfection which was ever present to their minds,—the noble conception of a personal self-existent God, infinite in power and wisdom, in holiness and majesty,—did operate most powerfully to elevate, expand, and purify their souls. So far as the mass of the nation were able to receive and entertain such views, and were believingly familiar with them, the same effects must have been wrought on them.

Here, then, as before, we ask, What explanation shall be given? With the indisputable fact before us, that a belief in a living personal God has proved itself in every age and nation most salutary in its influence on human character; that its tendency has clearly been to develop intellectual and moral life and energy, and to invest humanity with the charms of moral loveliness, are we to think—can we imagine—that this belief is without the least foundation—a fond but idle fancy—an empty, vain delusion? Who has credulity enough for this? Who can persuade himself that this grand moral force which has been seen exerting itself on the minds and hearts of men from the creation until now, is after all a mere nonentity—a fiction of the mind itself? This striking fact, that the influence of a belief in the divine existence has always been so eminently happy and ennobling, must make the supposition that this belief is false, seem utterly absurd to the candid, thoughtful mind.

You will observe, that in calling your attention to the several important facts to which we have referred, it has not been asserted that any one of them, or even all of them together, do constitute an absolute and perfect demonstration of a God. On the contrary, we have said that such a thing is not to be expected. But what we say is this. The human mind, whenever and wherever developed into intelligent consciousness, appears naturally and necessarily to have the notion of a God. The more reflective, and especially the more virtuous men have been in every age, the more as the general rule they have loved and cherished this idea. Those who, for any reason, have sought to rid themselves of all belief in God, have found the task extremely difficult—almost impossible. The conception of a universe without a God is, when deliberately considered, naturally abhorrent to the soul. And, finally, the belief in a self-conscious, intelligent, personal Deity, has always been seen to exert the best influence on human character and happiness. Each one of these facts, considered by itself, is wholly unaccountable except on the supposition that God actually exists. Each one of them impresses the serious, honest mind with a conviction of his being; and then, when we take them all together—with no conflicting proof to neutralize their force—they carry that conviction to a moral certainty, which sound philosophy, and the laws of reasoning on such subjects, decide to be not at all less satisfactory and conclusive, than that of the most rigid demonstration. Such is the method, and such the result of the present argument. It is only one of several modes in which we may consider this great subject. We may take other stand-points, and have recourse to other kinds of proof; and so, as we observed in the beginning, we may confirm our moral instincts by substantial arguments adduced in indefinite accumulation.

Let us also understand that the study of this subject is not unprofitable speculation. Far from it. Scepticism, so often repulsed in its grosser attacks on divine religion, has in this, our time, assumed a more refined and subtle form. The philosophical pantheism of the schools of Germany and of the most recent sceptical writers of England and America, is a practical if not a real atheism. If God be not a living, personal, self-conscious being, existing apart fróm the creation, but only an unconscious necessary cause or force evolving itself in the universe of things and always immanent in it, the name may be retained, but the thing is gone for ever. Such a necessary cause, or force, or ground of being—call it what you will—is no more God in any proper sense than was the eternal fate of the Greek mythology. The advocates of the modern pantheistic views do as completely empty the universe of God, according to any true notion of his being, as it is possible to do; and leave an awful vacancy as horrible to the conception of a healthful, sober mind, as it was represented in the passage quoted from Jean Paul a little while ago.

Yet these are the views which in so many captivating

forms, in books and lectures, in poetry and prose, are now addressed to the better class of minds among the young people of our land. Their vagueness takes the imagination. Their pretension excites the hope of augmented light. But, believe it, they do but mock with empty names, and with bewildering shadows; and bring, instead of increased illumination, the murky gloom of unalleviated darkness—

"Black as deep midnight, terrible as hell!"

From all such exhibitions turn to the facts affirmed by human consciousness and human history, to which we have referred, and let them make their mighty plea for God—the real God—within your souls. It is clear, with such facts before you, that your souls are made to conceive of God; that they deeply yearn for God; that they cleave to a belief in God; that they shrink from the orphanage to which his non-existence would consign them; and finally, that they feel themselves drawn upward in the scale of being by the glorious attraction of his infinite perfection. You must then recognise the living God. You cannot do without him. The planets in the heavens, which are held ever in their places by the attraction of the central orb, and have all their life and gladness in his beams, shall as soon be able to do without the sun, as you shall be able to do without the centre of all minds, the resplendent light of all the universe, the fountain of those influences and those attractions, which produce and perpetuate throughout the whole, order, harmony, and blessedness. There is a God. It is only the fool that denies it in his heart.

VI.

Argument from Design for the Divine Existence.

ROM. i. 20 : *For the invisible things of Him, from the creation of the world are clearly seen, being understood by the things that are made, even his eternal power and Godhead.*

IN a former discourse we have endeavoured to present the evidence of the divine existence which is furnished by the moral constitution, instincts, and history of man, as exhibited in certain familiar and generally admitted facts. It was then observed that that was only one of many lines of argument which might properly be pursued, for the purpose of advancing the instinctive belief in the being of a God which men seem naturally to entertain, to a full conviction of the understanding—a rational faith, logically established by conclusive proofs.

The text invites us to take another position and to pursue another course of thought on this deeply interesting subject. In order to render its exact meaning a little more easy to be apprehended, we may paraphrase this remarkable passage in the following manner:—For his invisible attributes, even his eternal power and divinity, are clearly seen since the creation of the world, being rendered intelligible by the things that are made. I propose, in this discourse, to direct your thoughts to the truth which it clearly states,—that *the constitution and the phenomena of the system of nature afford decisive evidence of the existence of a God.*

The argument constructed on this basis is what is commonly called the argument from design. Kant and his followers among the Germans, and Coleridge and those who adopt his views among English and American writers on the subject, have denied the validity of this argument; or rather they have denied that it amounts to a strict and absolute demonstration—a thing which ought never to have been claimed in its behalf. It is an argument of the moral or probable kind; and as such, when correctly stated, it is not only valid and worthy of attention, but is in fact one of the most striking and irresistible that can be presented to the mind. The mind being, as we have seen, instinctively disposed to find a God, the constitution and aspects of nature attentively and candidly considered, afford it proofs of his existence, which though not mathematically demonstrative in their nature, are yet, if allowed their fair impression, not at all inferior, in their power to produce conviction, to the severest demonstration.

The argument, in short, is this. The system of nature exhibits innumerable instances of the adaptation of means to ends and of particular and general design. We are certain that this system had a beginning. To originate it, there must have been a contriver and architect adequate to the production of such a universe; and although as the universe is not infinite, an infinite designer is not mathematically proved, yet as the mind is constituted, it cannot conceive of a being capable of producing such a universe, without feeling it absurd to set any limits to his power, and wisdom, and other manifested attributes; without, in a word, ascribing to Him the attributes which constitute a personal God of infinite perfection. We are not to consider what would be the force of this evidence apart from the peculiar laws of our moral nature; but what is its legitimate and actual force as addressed to such a nature. Considered in its relation to our minds, particularly to our moral instincts, the proof of a God derived from the appearances of nature is certainly clear and satisfactory. That this may appear, we will more fully illustrate and amplify the argument as just stated in a brief and simple way.

Suppose, then, that in travelling through a country in which you are a stranger, you arrive at a splendid palace. You observe, as you approach it, that the noble park in which it is embosomed, is carefully enclosed, that it is adorned with a variety of trees, many of them obviously transplanted from foreign climes, and that herds of deer are grazing on its slopes. Its gardens, you notice, are planned in exact accordance with the rules of correct perspective, and are supplied with every plant and shrub recommended either by utility or beauty, and with the choicest fruits of all the several seasons. The edifice itself strikes you at once as a model of architectural symmetry and proportion, and as in all respects exceedingly well-planned. On its top is an observatory, furnished with a telescope ingeniously arranged, and commanding the most delightful views in all directions. As you ascend the marble steps, which are hewn and laid with mathematical exactness, and the door balanced nicely on its hinges, opens at your touch, you perceive that throughout the whole establishment there is perfect order, combined with admirable taste and art. The hall is large and airy, and enriched with the master-pieces of the painter and the sculptor; the drawing-rooms are lofty and well-proportioned, while the brilliant chandelier dependent from the ceiling and the massive lamps upon the mantel, furnish complete facilities for the most agreeable illumination. You find also in their proper places the useful chair, the comfortable sofa, and the luxurious couch with its downy pillow. In short, after examining every part attentively, you can discover nothing wanting which could contribute to the comfort or the pleasure of the occupant.

After having satisfied your curiosity and admired sufficiently the wisdom which contrived and the skill which executed so fine a plan, you resume your journey anxious to be informed who has fitted up for himself this magnificent abode. Soon you meet a resident of the neighbourhood, and ask him to inform you. With an air of surprise at your inquiry he replies, "That palace was never built, as you suppose. It has *always* stood there precisely as it is." You feel the entire absurdity of such an answer, and conclude that your informant is a fool, or else that he believes that you are one. You meet a second and repeat your question. He gravely tells you that your impressions respecting it are wholly wrong; that there is really no contrivance or design about it; that matter must exist under some form or other; and that among the infinity of possible modifications it has happened to take the order and arrangement you have noticed. This answer you find even more repugnant to your reason than the former; and intent on coming at the truth, you ask a third. His statement is, that a man of princely means and tastes at a certain time selected the site of the palace, laid out and beautified the grounds, erected the noble edifice, procured the costly furniture, and spared no pains to make it a rich and convenient habitation, and that at particular seasons of the year he is wont to occupy it and to enjoy the means of happiness which it affords. This answer accords with all that you have seen, and is a satisfactory solution of the case.

Like such a palace is the natural world around you. Throughout its diversified and almost innumerable arrangements you see a design which evinces surprising wisdom and an execution indicative of boundless power. The globe itself is one of the members of a nicely adjusted system. For thousands of years it has moved through a path more than five hundred millions of miles in circuit, never wandering from its course. During the same period it has steadily revolved upon its axis, maintaining with undeviating regularity the alternations of day and night. Everywhere, on the surface of the earth, you find the animal, vegetable, and mineral kingdoms characterized by adaptations the most wonderful and perfect, and by a rigid conformity to law. There is a place and a use for everything, and everything is fitted to its place and use. Modify at any point the existing order of things, and you are certain to introduce disorder and deformity. Exchange, for example, the teeth and claws of the lion for the grinders and cloven feet of the ox, and the one would inevitably famish amid the mountains of prey, and the other though surrounded by the ample luxuriance of the pasture. Give to the eagle fins, and transfer his pinions to the shark, and each would perish hopelessly, unfitted for his proper element. For the grateful verdure of the grass and trees let there be substituted the bright yellow of the gold-cup or the pure white of the lily, or the dazzling scarlet of the geranium, and you might almost as well put out the sun, or at once doom all the world to blindness. Let the granite strata be transformed to diamond, and you could neither remove them from their places nor convert them to your use with any tolerable convenience. Let your springs of water lose their pure and grateful tastelessness, and acquire instead a sweet or a spicy flavour, and your drink would shortly cloy your appetite and beget a loathing. In a word, suppose any material change you please in the constitution of the natural world and you will find that mischievous results would inevitably follow its occurrence. It is a perfect and harmonious whole, uniting, like the palace in the case supposed, both usefulness and beauty, each in its due proportion.

But the fact that there are indications in the system of nature of a general plan, an adjustment of the several parts to one another, is not all that it concerns us to observe. Each natural object in itself, and aside from its relations to the whole, exhibits proof of wise contrivance and design. The vegetable and animal kingdoms perhaps furnish the most striking instances of this. The botanist who examines the germinating and fructifying organs of plants, and the anatomist who explores the mysteries of the animal economy, find at every step of their investigations adaptations which surprise by their ingenuity and astonish by their perfection. Many of these provisions, indeed, are obvious only to the scientific eye; yet very many also may be noticed by the most uninformed observer. Who, for instance, can have failed to mark how the seed of the thistle is scattered over the face of the earth by means of its balloon of down? Who has not noticed how the reed, the corn-stalk, and the tall spire of grass, could not have stood erect but for the singular device of joints formed at certain intervals, which add greatly to their strength? To whom has it not occurred that to invert the position of the ear would be almost to destroy its value? Who has not often admired the position and the structure of that most perfect of all telescopes—the eye? Defended by the nasal, cheek, and frontal bones, and veiled by its elastic curtain, delicate as it is, it is probably more rarely injured than any other organ; while with its complicated lenses, its dilating and contracting pupil, and its self-regulating power, it is a specimen of unrivalled mechanism. We might go on to mention the heart, with its cells, and valves, and spontaneous motion—the lungs, with their delicate and elastic structure—and the limbs, with their muscles, tendons, ligaments, and joints. But it is not my design to pursue this part of the subject into minute detail.

Now to the question that forces itself upon every thoughtful mind—whence this obvious general design, and these wonderful special adaptations, one of three answers must be given—namely, Either things have always existed as they are; or they exist in their present state by accident; or they are the work of an intelligent Author.

The first of these answers—that the world has always existed as it is—corresponds, you perceive, with the reply of the person whom we supposed to say that the palace so complete and well-arranged was never built, but had always presented the appearance described; and the falsehood of the one is not less palpable than that of the other. There is, on the first mention of the thing, the same sort of difficulty in conceiving of such a world without a planner as such an edifice without an architect; and then, further, whatever may or may not be true about the eternity of matter, we positively know—for science, particularly the science of geology, affords most ample proof of the fact—that the present system of things upon our earth is not eternal. It has not always existed as it is, but has had a comparatively recent origin. The several stages or gradations by which it has reached its present state are written for our study on the successive strata of the rocks. With the testimony of the sciences all the existing records of human history agree. While the remains of perished genera and species, both of animals and plants, declare that neither of these departments of nature has been always as it is, there are abundant facts to prove that the human race have not always existed on the earth.

I omit on this point some abstract modes of reasoning,

which have commonly been employed, as rendered unnecessary by the facts to which we have just referred.

The second answer, which corresponds with the reply supposed in our illustration—that the palace was produced fortuitously as one possible form of matter—assumes that matter has inherent in it some blind force—some tendency to organized arrangement, by virtue of which, in the course of ages, it has assumed the forms in which we see it. On this we may remark that the assumption is wholly conjectural and unsupported. There is not the slightest proof of such a tendency to organize; but, on the contrary, natural philosophy lays it down as a fundamental doctrine that matter is entirely passive—that is, that if put at rest it remains at rest, and if put in motion it remains in motion. But even if such a tendency were granted, it would transcend belief entirely that a mere blind property of matter should produce contrivance so ingenious and workmanship so exquisite, that the most perfect human sagacity and skill cannot rival it by an immeasurable distance. Then, further, it is not material forms alone which are to be accounted for, but also the vital principle in all organic life, and the intelligence exhibited by the animal creation, and most of all by man. To suppose these things to result from the mere juxtaposition of material particles, is to exhibit the credulity of believing without the slightest evidence, and to rest our opinions upon fancy.

We are shut up, therefore, to the third alternative—to the conclusion that, like the palace, our world must have been contrived and fitted up by a wise designer. After surveying its broad plan, and observing how it bears, even in its minutest parts, the most indubitable marks of intelligent adaptation, the mind can find no resting-place but in the admission of a personal Creator, endowed with the power, the wisdom, and other attributes, whatever they may be, which render him adequate to the work of constructing and sustaining such a system; and then when we enlarge our view and take in the vast extent of the creation, of which the amazing discoveries of astrononical science give us only a faint idea, we perceive that a being adequate to the work of creating, upholding, and governing such a universe, must be so great, so transcendant in his attributes, that we can form no higher conception of infinity, or of absolute perfection, than is realized in him. To minds constituted like ours, it matters not that the proof of an infinite, self-conscious, living God is not demonstrative in its nature; it is enough that to a soul instinctively demanding such a God it carries the presumption that there is such a being up to the highest point of moral certainty, and thus authorizes and sustains the most complete conviction.

The argument for the divine existence from the adaptation and design which are apparent must, however, in order to be complete, be carried forward from the aspects of the natural world as observed by the intelligent mind, to the constitution and the phenomena which the mind itself exhibits. In the general adaptation of the soul of man to its position and relations, in the fitness of each particular faculty to its end, and the adjustment and harmony of the whole, there meet us the same indications of wisdom directed to purposes and ends which are so striking in material nature. The relation between the eye and the light, the lungs and the air, the ear and the atmospheric vibrations, is not more notable and significant than that of the intellect to the objects of knowledge, of the natural sensibilities to the causes of pleasure and pain, of the conscience to the impression of right and wrong, and of the desires and the will to the forms of good presented. We cannot here enter on any illustration of this part of the argument. The mode of reasoning is the same, whether we attend to matter or to mind. The inner world supplies us proofs of a designing God profoundly interesting, and, if possible, even more impressive, when carefully examined, than those of the world without. The common mind is most easily led to notice the marks of divine wisdom in material nature. But the facts which the world of mind presents are equally conclusive when once they are examined, as has of late been shown by several able writers.

To every enlightened and really honest mind, therefore, what the apostle asserts so distinctly in the text is manifestly true. The invisible attributes of God, even his eternal power and Godhead, are clearly seen since the creation of the world. Such a mind feels, that to refuse to admit this, is to resist the laws of evidence, is to do violence to its own urgent convictions, and to plunge into the most palpable absurdities. It seems impossible, indeed, that any person, with a healthful tone of moral feeling, should bring himself to an honest, deliberate conclusion that there is no God, after having intelligently studied nature or himself. The irreligious man may say this in his heart; but he will still continue to see it written on every part of the fair fabric of creation—every house is builded by some man, but he that built all things is God! Yes, every star that sparkles in the firmament; every planet as it rolls; the moon as she walks in brightness, and the sun as he travels in his strength; each with its own emphatic voice declares there is a God! Every seed that germinates, every flower that blooms, every fruit that ripens, every leaf of the forest that trembles in the breeze, tells us there is a God! Every eye that sees, every ear that hears, every heart that throbs, every bird that flies through the midst of heaven, every fish that roams through the ocean's caves, and every beast upon a thousand hills, declares there is a God! And lastly, every mind that thinks, and wills, and reasons, and remembers, and feels the sense of moral obligation, most impressively of all, gives testimony to the existence and perfections of a divine Creator.

> "Here is firm footing, here is solid rock,
> And all is sea besides."

Here we may rest unmoved. This truth admitted, the universe is harmonized; much of its darkness is dispelled, and a key is furnished for the solution of many of its mysteries. If there yet remain anomalies which baffle us, if there are some arrangements whose design we are thus far unable to discover, if there are still deeps which we cannot fathom with our utmost reach of intellect, let us remember that our understanding bears a less relation to the Infinite Intelligence, than a grain of sand bears to the material universe; and in faith and meekness let us wait, till we shall be placed in that higher world, where with expanded intellect and clearer vision, we shall behold the glory of the Lord.

If now, it be true, that the appearances of nature do plainly teach that there is a Supreme Being, then certainly it follows that all mankind are bound to recognise him. Paul, in the context, is speaking of the heathen; and he declares that even their ignorance of God is without excuse. It is an ignorance which exists in spite of evidence, and is fostered by depravity. There is no corner of the world so dark that the rays of the divine glory are not reflected there from the face of the Creation; no eye is so blind that it could not discern them by attentive observation.

But if the least enlightened are under obligation to know God from his works, much more are they whose minds have been educated to reflect, and to whom science has laid open the mysteries of nature. If such assert that they can see no proofs of a Creator, can it be otherwise than true that they are either flagrantly dishonest, or pitifully weak. If they are not so near to idiocy as to be unable to understand the connection between effects and causes, can they be otherwise than wholly inexcusable, if they do not habitually and with full conviction, recognise the divine existence. When the voice of universal nature cries, "There is a God!" our inmost souls must heartily respond, "There is a God!"

And while nature, by the light which she imparts respecting God, lays on us the obligation to acknowledge him, she also binds us to adore him. It is obvious to reflect, that he whose power was adequate to the creation of what our eyes behold must be almighty. The wisdom which devised this wondrous mechanism, and these countless forms of beauty, must be imagined to be infinite. The benevolence which has displayed itself to such an extent in the production of what is good, should certainly be presumed to be unimpeachable, even if in a few particulars the harmony of things should not be clearly seen. And can we know a being whose power and wisdom and benevolence are boundless, and not be under obligation to regard him with reverence and affection? He appears most worthy of our homage and our love; if, therefore, we withhold it, we manifestly rob him of his right. All that is sublime in greatness, all that is grand in intellect, and all that is admirable in excellence, is blended into ineffable glory in his character as thus exhibited; and if we fail to think of him with reverence, and to contemplate his perfections with delight, we clearly evince that sin has vitiated our moral tastes, has perverted and debased the best affections of our souls.

See to it, then, that you make God a living reality to your daily apprehension. Be more observing of his works, more watchful of his providence, and more anxious to learn by every means all that you can learn respecting him. Let the truth that there is a God not only not be questioned, but not lost sight of for a moment. When you lie down, and when you rise up, when you sit in the house, and when you walk by the way, let it be ever present to your thoughts. Let it comfort you in sorrow, and chasten the excitement of your joy. If you are tempted to go in the ways of sin, let it ring in your ears like a voice of terror; and if you are treading in the paths of holiness, let it strengthen and make glad your souls. Let nothing tempt you to listen to the suggestions of scepticism even for a moment. To yield up the mind to them is virtually to shut your eyes, and to stop your ears, and with the perverseness of deliberate folly to plunge into the blackness of darkness. Atheism can shed no ray of comfort on the soul. It throws a pall over the glories of the universe, and shrouds all things in funereal gloom. Take away from me the evidence that there is a God, and show me that I am only a product of necessity or chance, without a Father, and without the hope of that divine sympathy for which my heart is yearning, and I will sit down and weep through the little that remains of life, and wish that I had never waked to conscious being. But so long as I can look over the broad earth, and the heaving sea, and the azure firmament, and see it written there that God exists, I will rejoice in my own existence, and will feel that there is a sun to illuminate the universe, and to diffuse throughout it light, and life, and blessedness! And since my reason teaches me to believe without a question that—

> If there's a power above us—
> He must delight in virtue,
> And that which he delights in must be happy,—

it shall be the great end of all my thoughts to study his perfections, and in my humble measure to attain his moral image!

VII.

The Christian Revelation to be Presumed Divine.

2 Peter i. 16: *For we have not followed cunningly devised fables.*

THE existence of God admitted, another question at once suggests itself. Has this divine Being directly revealed himself and made known his will to man? Of course, if he be recognised as the Author of nature, that must be acknowledged to be an expression of his thought, and, so far as it goes, an illustration of his attributes and character. By the careful study of this, to the extent of our faculties and time, we might expect to arrive at some practical conclusions as to what course of conduct on our part would be in accordance with his will, and would best promote our own welfare. But has he been pleased to instruct men *supernaturally?* Apart from the lessons taught by the constitution of the world and the orderly on-goings of the great system of natural causes, has he come to the intelligent soul of man with immediate inspirations of his own wisdom, and as if with words from his own lips?

We were taught in childhood that he has. We have believed it, without hesitation, up to that point at which we are led to reflect on all our principal beliefs, and to ask on what they rest. Now doubts arise, and we feel the necessity of deliberate examination. In this period of thoughtful inquiry it is of the first importance that we should approach the subject, not only with a candid and honest spirit, with entire openness to conviction, but also with a just view of the position of the question. In regard to most inquiries in the region of practical truth, it is found that, on the first proposal of them, there is something to give the mind a prepossession in one way or another; something which begets a presumption either for a particular conclusion, or against it. The cause of this bias may lie, not in the subject, but in the state of the mind itself; in its tastes, desires, or previous modes of thinking. However it may be accounted for, it has too generally happened that those who have been led to doubt the reality of divine revelation, and have set themselves to examine the matter, have come to the inquiry with a conviction, or at least a feeling, that the presumption at the outset is *against* the claim that a positive revelation has been made. Of course, the evidence demanded must be of sufficient force to overcome this unfavourable state of mind, as well as to convince the understanding.

The truth, we insist, is, in fact, directly the reverse of this very common impression of the doubting. We desire to show in the present discourse, and hope to make it appear conclusively, that to a candid inquirer, who *now* comes to a consideration of the subject, there is a strong antecedent presumption *in favour* of that professed revelation which claims our credence in the Bible; that such a person is justified in assuming that, aside from its immediate and proper proofs, there is a high probability that these received deliverances of God to men are genuine and true.

Without going into the philosophical question of the conceivable possibility of a revelation, or inquiring as to the reality of the miracles, and prophecies, and testimonies, by which it claims to be authenticated, we say first of all, that the very existence of this alleged revelation, in the form in which we find it, affords a presumption of its truth.

The first thing that strikes one on glancing at the books of the Old and New Testament, in which what is called the Christian revelation is contained, is the exceedingly heterogeneous character of their contents. They present a collection of the writings of a great number of persons, scattered through a long course of ages, of various social grades, from the condition of herdsmen and fishermen to that of eminent statesmen and illustrious sovereigns; of different sorts of talent, of dissimilar tastes, habits, and culture, and, to a great extent, unconnected with each other. The styles of composition are as diverse as the authors. There are genealogies, geographical and ethnological details, fragmentary and connected histories; poetry, including the pastoral, the psalm, the anthem, the war-song, the elegy, the drama, and the highest range of the descriptive and impassioned; biographies and pictures of social life and manners, proverbs, discourses, precepts, parables, letters. What a medley! one might naturally exclaim on first looking at the volume. A little of all ages, of all sorts of men, and of all varieties of human thought! This, regarding them simply as authentic writings, and just as you regard Herodotus and Livy, Plato and Seneca, Pindar and Horace.

But on even a cursory reading of these writings, heterogeneous as they seem, you cannot fail to be equally impressed with a second fact about them—this, namely, that they have, after all, a strange and most striking unity. One spirit breathes throughout the whole. The same conception of God, as the eternal, self-existent, and infinite Creator, of his natural government of the world, and of his moral government of rational creatures; the same general notions of right and wrong; the same views of the design of human existence, of the individual responsibility of men, of the blessedness of well-doing and of the miseries of sin; of the guilt and want of mankind, of the justice, the goodness, and the grace of God, and of the way of reconciliation with him. Nor does this unity of sentiment, of spirit, and of general scope and purpose seem less, but rather greater, the more carefully and thoroughly these various compositions are examined. With all the diversities naturally resulting from the fact that each writer exhibits the peculiar characteristics of his own genius, age, country, language, and personal condition, and notwithstanding that the books of the several authors were published independently of each other, these writings are so entirely alike in their moral tone, and so completely harmonious in their presentations of the cardinal truths of religion, that they appear as if originally designed to make one perfect whole when brought together, like the separate beams in the framework of a building. No competent person can attentively read the Christian Scriptures, whatever may be his opinion about their origin, without perceiving that there is one continuous stream of thought and feeling flowing down throughout the whole, from the earliest to the latest, varying only in this, that it grows deeper and broader by frequent homogenous accessions as it sweeps onward through the ages.

Here, then, is an undeniable fact to be accounted for. Through this line of individual men, posted at various intervals back to the beginning of the world, there have been transmitted certain distinctive views of God and religion, which out of this line have come to us from no other portion of the race. That these men have not been mere copyists from each other, the specific diversities, and the accessions and progressive development of thought to which we have referred, afford decisive proof. Two questions meet us therefore, namely, How came they, any of them, by views at once so unique in themselves and so immeasurably superior in intellectual and moral elevation to those attained by the historians, the poets, and the sages of all the world besides? And then, how came they, writing separately and each for his own particular end, living also some of them centuries and even thousands of years apart, so to harmonize with and to supplement each other, that taken together their writings form one grand and well-adjusted whole? We will not now assert that with these questions before us the conviction must arise that there is something supernatural in all this, and that these men must have been the instruments by which a real positive revelation has been made; but certainly it is saying very little to say that the facts of the case, if candidly considered, do justify us in approaching the Bible, do demand even that we approach it, with a strong presumption that it is what it purports to be—the word of the living God supernaturally conveyed to men. If each of the authors of the sacred books, in his own age, for his own ends, and without the least relation to the others, had wrought a piece of brass into a given form; and if at last, when these pieces were all collected and compared, it had been found that they together formed a perfect piece of mechanism, a watch for instance, the impression of a superhuman agency directing the whole matter would hardly have been stronger than it now actually is.

The presumption thus created by the existence of the Christian revelation in the form in which we find it, is greatly strengthened, we have further to observe, by the obvious and admitted fact that it has entered most profoundly into the life and thought of the world. This current of professed revelation, that, like a river flowing through many lands and climes, has held its way through the revolutions of centuries and the countless vicissitudes of human affairs, has not been an insulated thing, a mere object of attention and of interest. As the waters are not confined within the river banks, but penetrate the bordering lands, ascend in vapour to fall again in showers, and thus enter with their vitalizing power the domain of vegetable life—so what have claimed to be the truths received from heaven have entered into and permeated the heart of humanity to a wonderful extent, and exhibit themselves in all history, in the thought, the learning, the institutions, the enterprises, and the aspirations of the most enlightened and vigorous portions of the race.

We are not here giving an opinion, let it be remembered, but merely stating a fact familiar to every one acquainted with history and with the ideas that enter into our modern civilization. It has been true, according to all historical records, and all the surviving literature of past ages, that a belief in the unity of God and in his providential government of the world—a belief which, wherever it has existed, has exhibited its power to elevate human character and thought—has never been held consistently and steadily, except along with a prevailing faith in revelation. It is equally obvious that the doctrines in regard to the rights of man which have for centuries been working their way in the most enlightened States; which are steadily mitigating social evils, raising to a higher level the masses of the people, developing the sense of individual manhood and weakening the arm of the oppressor; which, either through institutions or through the force of public opinion, are exalting men to the responsibilities and benefits of civil and religious liberty;—it is true, I say, that these doctrines are to be traced to those views of the value, the accountability, the immortal nature and high destiny of individual man, which were originally delivered in the so-called sacred books, and have never been found to any considerable extent, except where these are found. If it were possible to eliminate from the structure of modern civilized society all the elements derived directly or indirectly from these, to withdraw them would be to take away what is most vital, most distinctive, most noble, and most hopeful as regards the future of humanity. The very men who profess now to reject revealed religion, would cling with all tenacity to fundamental truths and principles pertaining to God, to man, and to society, which have been derived alone from the professed records of revelation. To this it must be added, that all departments of the literature of the most cultivated nations—history, eloquence, poetry, criticism, and even fiction—as well as the higher fields of science and philosophy, are interfused with elements of thought, of taste, of imagination, and with notions that enter into and determine to no small extent, the modes of reasoning which are adopted, the source of which is undeniably the same. Whether the Bible be true or false the fact is before our eyes that its contents have entered profoundly into the mind and heart of humanity, and have to a great extent become blended with its intellect and sentiment alike.

Nor can it be said that other pretended systems of religion have done the same. There are no facts of history by which such an assertion can be justified. What claims to be the Christian revelation extends back to the beginning of the world, and covers the whole period of the world's life; always self-consistent, the same in essence, and changing only so far as change is necessarily implied in a progressive and orderly development. It has no parallel among the systems which have only existed for comparatively short periods, and have been subject to constant modifications of their essential character. It has reached a vastly larger portion of the race than any one of them. It has wrought far more deeply and effectively so far as it has extended. We have in this view, certainly, a good ground for presuming at once its reality and its intrinsic reasonableness and power.

Still further, a third fact lies before us in regard to the asserted Christian revelation, which, fairly considered, must predispose us to receive it. To the statement just made, that it has entered deeply into the world's life, we have to add, what is equally significant, that the effects which it has wrought, both on individual man and on society, have uniformly been salutary in a very eminent degree.

That the principles of action, the spirit insisted on, and the ends proposed in the Christian revelation are eminently pure and noble, the stoutest unbelief has never hesitated to acknowledge. That the influence of these things on those with whose minds and hearts they are brought in contact, must be very positive and eminently good, is of course a necessary conclusion from the nature of the case. The whole history of Christianity, and of Judaism as well, is rich, moreover, in illustration of its actual effects. Let it not be imagined that we are going about to show that faith in revelation has not been sometimes found asso- iated with ignorance and superstition, and individual and social degeneracy. We have no reluctance to the admission that it has. But what we state is, and no intelligent person can dispute it, that the fact is patent that these evils never have *resulted*, and never can *result*, from a belief in revelation and the legitimate influence of the truths professedly revealed. As Christianity has come in contact with mankind in all degrees of culture, it has been received by the ignorant, the superstitious, and the degraded. As its good influences can only operate in a gradual manner for the improvement of character, and as they are liable to be impeded in their action by accidental causes found in the particular outward condition of those who may enjoy them, it may often happen in the case of any individual or people, that although the process of improvement is steadily going forward, there are evils, great and obvious, which have not been reached as yet. Unless it appears that the evils referred to are the natural and proper fruit of the influence of the Christian Scriptures, or, at least, that this has no fitness nor tendency to effect their ultimate removal, their existence in connection with a belief in revelation, cannot rightfully create a prejudice against the claim of that revelation to be real and divine.

But while Christianity does not appear at any time to have delivered mankind at once and wholly, on the first reception of it, from the evils under the power of which it found them, the examples of its eminently salutary effects, on both individual and social character, are, in all periods of its history, abundant and acknowledged. When first preached among the polytheistic, licentious, and generally corrupt nations included in the Roman Empire, it ere long did what the few moralists and sages of antiquity had sought to do in vain; it gave a fatal blow to the popular idolatry, and, in spite of venerable associations, and splendid shrines, and captivating ceremonies, it brought the gods into general contempt, and left their temples to stand empty and deserted. Then out of the degenerate masses of the people it raised up vast multitudes, of both sexes, and of all ages and conditions, in whose lives the purest virtues, and in whose sufferings and deaths, in attestation of the sincerity and strength of their belief, the sternest and the noblest heroism were everywhere exhibited. All this on the testimony of secular and unfriendly historians, of imperial edicts and Roman annalists. The very highest instances of unpretending goodness, of unfaltering steadiness of principle, of generous self-sacrifice, of obedience to the sense of duty, of sublime courage to endure, are, by common consent, admitted to abound in the authentic records of the noble army of Christian martyrs and confessors. These, too, are allowed to be the proper products of Christianity, and not things incidentally connected with it.

It has sometimes seemed, to careless or superficial readers of history, that the state of the western nations of the old world during the middle ages, when Christianity had been established and generally diffused, was in conflict with the supposition of its elevating power. The dark ages, they observe, succeeded the early and widely-extended triumphs of the cross. Yes; but along with this we have another fact that stands in equal prominence beside it. The mighty deluge of barbarism that swept over the Roman Empire was sufficiently vast in its extent to engulf, as in the bosom of a mighty ocean, all the elements and forces of the existing civilization, and Christianity among the rest. Intellectual and moral twilight was a necessary consequence; and it could not have been otherwise than that a long period would be required in order that Christianity, operating simply as one restoring energy in the abysses of this vast chaos, might make itself distinctly seen and felt in its proper character and influence. No wonder that a little leaven, overwhelmed with a continent of meal, should be long in pervading the whole mass. That the influence of Christianity did much to mitigate and to remove the horrors of the medieval darkness, and that it has supplied many of the best ideas, activities, and elevating forces of our modern civilization, are facts about which there is no dispute among those who are competent to offer an opinion. It is owing in no small measure, to state the matter very moderately, to the influence of Christianity, that humanity has so far emerged from its deep and long eclipse.

It must be noted, too, that in the activity of that new life and free expansion to which Christianity has again attained, especially within the present century, she is producing in the sight of all men the same wonderful transformations of individual and social character, the same spirit of benevolence, the same noble charities, the same antagonism to evil, the same hopes and labours for the welfare of mankind, the same virtues, culture, and refinement, and the same sober, intelligent, and healthful piety, as in her early days. Never was it more manifest than now that the legitimate fruits of the Christian revelation are eminently salutary, are contributing richly to the well-being of the world. Can it be otherwise than rational to presume that such a professed revelation will prove on examination to be genuine?

Not less significant is a fourth fact which presents itself at the outset to the inquirer about the Christian revelation. It has thus far stood secure against all assaults of those who have sought to overthrow it, although these assaults have been many, persistent, and often conducted with great ability and learning. Nothing pertaining to the past is better known than that the attempt to storm the citadel of revelation has been repeated till it seems to have been assailed at every point; and that it still remains uncarried we have the witness of our own eyes and ears.

The ancient prophets, each in his turn, encountered the resistance of unbelief. They were charged with prophesying falsely in the name of God; of arrogating to themselves the office and authority of religious teachers, and wishing to secure a pre-eminence of influence. They suffered persecution and sometimes death at the hands of those who denied their divine authority. Yet their teachings lived, and gained and kept a place in the hearts of multitudes. When Jesus of Nazareth appeared and claimed to be the predicted Messiah and the Redeemer and Light of the world, a corrupt Judaism expressed the strength of its hostility, the venom of its hate, by nailing him, as if a malefactor, to the cross. When the apostles and the primitive disciples began at Jerusalem the preaching of the word, they too were met with an equally determined and virulent opposition from those who, because not understanding their own Scriptures, did not perceive that Christianity was but the full development of the faith delivered to their fathers. Yet steadily the Christian doctrines won their way.

Then followed the long and mighty struggle between

Christianity and the prevailing systems of philosophy and religion throughout the Roman empire. It was a contest of life and death. From the nature of the case there could be no compromise, no truce. The new must exterminate the old, or the old the new. On every ground on which there seemed to be any hope of making a stand against the advancing Christian faith, a stand was made. At every point imagined to be vulnerable the system was pressed with direct attack. Whatever might be done by the civil power to resist and crush the Christian religion, was done with unflinching determination and barbarity, not only by the steady policy of the government, but by those horrible and repeated seasons of persecution during which the earth was deluged with martyr blood. Whatever might be achieved or hoped in the same direction by the use of the pen, was attempted by learned and able writers, such as Lucian, Celsus, Porphyry, Hierocles, and others, who, not content with a defence of the popular beliefs, assailed the religion of Christ with argument and ridicule, with misrepresentation and abuse. Yet, after all, the Christian faith held on its way and triumphed.

So it has been in the modern world. The wits, philosophers, and savans of France, in the last century, having resolved, in a spirit of implacable hostility, to exterminate all faith in the Christian revelation, assailed it with pungent satire, with the coarsest ribaldry, with caricatures introduced into the drama, and all the current forms of popular literature, with the subtlety and acuteness of philosophy, and with weapons alleged to be furnished by the discoveries of modern science. English Deism, in a higher style of thought, with greater strength of reasoning, with no little real learning, enlisting champions who, to great metaphysical acumen, added untiring patience and fixed determination, attacked the historical credit, the supernatural credentials, and the asserted revelations of the Christian Scriptures. There was no lack of will, or talent, or diligent endeavour, for the entire demolition of the venerable structure of truth accepted as from heaven. Germany, with her unrivalled scholarship, her unflinching boldness, her amazing keenness of analysis and tenuity of thought, and her adventurous criticism, has so put to the torture the historic records and the peculiar doctrines of Christianity, as to make it impossible to conceive that any more formidable trial can await them. And, finally, the latest forms of German unbelief have flowed into the channels of English and American thought, and now for several years have been making demonstrations against the popular faith in a positive revelation.

What then is the result? Has the idea of a divine revelation come to be scouted generally either by the most intelligent and the best thinkers, or by the great mass of ordinary people? Has a single pillar of Christianity, by common acknowledgment, been removed out of its place? Has one entrenchment undeniably been carried, or one battery silenced, or one breastwork left in ruins? Who affirms this? Who believes it? It is doubtless true, that now, as always, there are some who reject revealed religion. But it is equally obvious that the vast majority of all who have at any time heartily believed Christianity, believe it still, nay more, believe it the more intelligently and strongly because of the fierce assaults through which it has been passing. Observe we are not asserting that Christianity is true, we are simply calling attention to the fact that unbelief, though it has made the attempt so often and with all imaginable weapons, *has not yet proved it false,* nor even weakened its hold upon the mind and heart of that part of the human race who have once intelligently received it. Approaching Christianity to-day as an inquirer in relation to its truth, I see it standing, not shattered and tottering by the multiplied assaults of ages, but as yet unharmed and safe ; a Malakoff, that hitherto has proved impregnable ; or better still, a grand old rock that, lying in mid-ocean, and beaten by mighty surges through successive centuries, still lifts its untroubled head in stern, yet calm repose. Is it not natural, then, since such I find it, that I should come to this professedly divine religion, with a strong presumption arising in my heart that what it claims to be I shall actually find it when I have thoroughly examined ?

We will note but one thing more. It is a fact which no one tolerably informed as to the condition and movements of the religious world will question, that at no period of its history was Christianity more vital, more powerful, more expectant and progressive, than at the present time. There may have been an intenser earnestness and loftier courage in the day of her primitive conquests ; but then she was weak in numbers and resources. To-day, her host is vast in multitude. In *position* she is strong ; for she is openly recognised by the public sentiment of the most enlightened nations of the earth, and her principles are inwrought to a very great extent into the governments and laws, the institutions, the policies, the social life, in short, into the entire structure of civilization, by which these nations are distinguished. How vast the amount of genius and learning enlisted in her service! How large a portion of literature, and art, and science is penetrated with her spirit! How immense the wealth at her command! How extensive and available her opportunities and means of bringing her influence to bear upon the world! Within the last half century she seems to have awaked to new activity, and to have girded up her loins for more extended and energetic action. Converts to her are multiplied by hundreds of thousands in a single year, and these not converts of the head only, but of the heart. Her sacred books are translated into all the chief languages of men. Her efforts are more than ever directed to the elevation and purification of social life, and the recovery of the world to goodness, by the universal application of her forces. Her plans are broad as the world. Her heralds are found in the remote islands of the sea, and in the centre of continents long covered with thick darkness. The force of habit is coming to strengthen the religious sentiment and conviction of her disciples, and to give steadiness and power to their exertions. The success of her domestic and foreign missionary enterprises, are stimulating her courage and inspiring her with hope. God, in his providence, finally, has done so much to remove the obstacles that in past ages checked her progress, that her expansive energy is now almost literally working without obstruction.

All this I see, you see, and all men see on every side. This life, and vigour, and progressive energy of the system of religion which rests on that professed revelation begun in the early ages of the world and completed in the days of Christ and his apostles, is certainly a most noticeable fact. It cannot but make a strong impression on every one who thoughtfully regards it. Can falsehood be imagined to have such vitality? Could anything but truth have so sustained itself through the revolving cycles of the past, that while empires, and dynasties, and cities, and monuments, and even literatures have perished, this should still seem as fresh as if immortal, and as full of activity and power as if in youth? Could anything have maintained so permanent a hold on the intellect and heart of the human race, a hold still growing firmer and giving promise of ultimate ascendency, which itself was without reality, a mere chimera? It will surely be admitted that taking what is called the Christian revelation as I find it, living, operative, and steadily extending the circle of its influence, while I bear in mind its history, there does appear to be a very strong presumption that its claims to be divine are just, before I begin to examine directly its credentials.

Remember, then, that so much as this is settled. When doubts have been excited, and you would seriously inquire as to the truth of the Christian revelation, you have no right, at this period of Christian history, to assume that the probability is all against it, and to call on Christianity to furnish proofs that may convince you, while in such a state of mind, beyond all cavil. She has her proper credentials, doubtless, if she be indeed from heaven, and she will not hesitate to show them. But since the facts of her ancient origin, of her perpetual power, of her salutary influence, of her steadfastness amidst attacks, and of her present vigour and advancing growth, create so strong a presumption in her favour, she is fairly entitled to take the benefit of her position. She may rightfully throw the burden of proof on you. She may demand, with justice, that you shall *admit* her claims until *you shall be able conclusively and finally to overthrow them;* until you can rationally account for her origin and character, her progressive life and action,—in short, for all the wonderful phenomena of her past and present existence. When you shall have seriously attempted this, you will have put yourself in a position to appreciate the proofs direct and positive, which she will then hold herself prepared to offer you.

Deal fairly, then, when you approach with your inquiries the Christian revelation. You see at a glance how venerable it is—going back for its beginnings to the morning of the world. You know that in its light, and hope, and inspiration, humanity has been exalted, intellect and genius quickened, art and science born, individual and social life ennobled, and truth and justice, benevolence and moral virtue in all forms, promoted among men. You have it in certain knowledge, that millions of the wisest, the greatest, and the best of earth—millions of the poor, the sorrowful, the oppressed—millions of every capacity, condition, and age, have found in heartily believing it new life and pure affections, a solid inward peace, tranquillity amidst life's fiercest storms, and deep serenity of soul, or joyful exultation, in the darkness and agony of death. Admit, then, to yourself, that, with all these facts before you, the presumption is so strong in favour of its truth, that it is most unreasonable to ask for such an amount and kind of immediate proof as would leave no possibility of cavil. Enough if it be found sustained by evidence which must convince and satisfy a truly honest and impartial mind.

Consider, too, that if the Christian revelation, as it has been received for ages, is divine, it must be the greatest of misfortunes to reject it as a fable. If it be indeed a sun kindled of God to illuminate the moral darkness of our world, it will shine on to cheer, and warm, and bless the happy multitudes who welcome it, though you shall avert your eyes and hide from its beams in the thick shades of unbelief. You have nothing—nothing—to gain if it be false. You have everything to hope for life, for death, for an immortality beyond, if, as you have been taught from childhood to believe, it is indeed a real utterance, a precious gift of the everliving God to man. May God enable every one of you to say with full conviction, "The word of God is heard in the Christian Scriptures. For we have not followed cunningly devised fables!"

VIII.

Christianity Authenticated in the Experience of its Power.

JOHN vi. 67–69: *Then said Jesus unto the twelve, Will ye also go away? Then Simon Peter answered him, Lord, to whom shall we go? Thou hast the words of eternal life. And we believe and are sure that thou art that Christ, the Son of the living God.*

AMONG those who attended on the ministry of Christ there were found, it appears, two sorts of professed disciples. There were some who were ready to attach themselves to him as followers, that were disciples of the understanding merely. They had observed his personal character. They had been struck with the extraordinary wisdom of his teachings. They had witnessed many of his mighty works, and had listened to the expositions he had given of many passages in the prophets as pointing to himself. On the whole, it seemed to them that the evidence of his Messiahship preponderated; and they were inclined to reckon themselves as his adherents.

The other class were, in some degree at least, disciples of the Spirit. With views of his character and mission as yet exceedingly defective in some particulars, they nevertheless felt the divine power of the doctrines which he taught. In the consciousness which they found deep within themselves that his words were indeed spirit and life to the soul, there was an inward witness that he came from heaven—the ground of a profound and heartfelt conviction that he was really the Christ of God.

There is nothing to excite surprise in the fact that those whose profession of discipleship was merely speculative and intellectual were brought to a stand, and even led to abandon Christ by difficulties. Their own power to understand what Jesus did and said was the measure of their faith. So long as they saw and heard nothing which they did not seem to themselves to comprehend—nothing which puzzled and perplexed them—they were ready to admit his claims. But when he uttered in their hearing truths which were so spiritual and so repugnant to their sensuous apprehensions, as those which related to the receiving of his body and blood as the condition, and the elements of life, their understandings were confounded; and because of this, they forthwith turned back, and concluded that they had been deceived. This was entirely natural.

But in regard to those who were driven to attach themselves to Christ by an inward perception of something divine in his person and his ministry, and by the response which his teachings awakened in their own moral natures, the case was wholly different. The faith of these did not rest on mere convictions of the intellect. It had a far deeper and more certain ground. Because this was the fact; because their inmost hearts *felt* the divinity which was in Christ, and their moral natures recognised and witnessed to the certainty of what he taught, it was not possible that any difficulties should overturn their confidence and drive them from him. Their understandings might be baffled; strange mysteries, and even apparent impossibilities and contradictions, might confront them. But what then? After all, there remained a voice in their own consciousness, which gave decisive and persistent witness to the Messiahship of Christ, and to the truth of the doctrines he delivered; so that when the question was propounded as is related in the text—will *ye* also go away? —it was altogether natural that they should answer as they did, repelling the thought of such a thing at once. It was, for them, impossible not to feel that to turn away from Christ, whatever perplexities might press them for the moment, would be to act in known and flagrant opposition to the truth. They could not but believe what they themselves had felt as vital truth in their inmost souls. To go away from one who had the words of eternal life, and in regard to whom they were able to say, We believe and are sure that thou art that Christ, the Son of the living God, seemed nothing short of the most preposterous folly.

Here, then, we have presented to our thoughts a most important fact; this, namely, that those who really enter into the spirit of Christianity, and feel somewhat of its true impression on their souls, find, in their own experience of its power, the most conclusive and satisfying proof that it is indeed a divine religion. We wish, in the present discourse, to set forth this fact distinctly. It is no part of our purpose to undervalue the various other kinds of evidence on which the certainty of the Christian revelation rests; but simply to insist that even leaving these aside, the gospel in itself—in its own peculiar power and life—does carry directly to the soul that cordially receives it, the undeniable credentials of divinity; does generate within an experimental consciousness in which there is good and sufficient warrant for a firm, unfaltering faith—a faith which places the suggestion of an abandonment of Christ in the light of a sheer absurdity.

First, then, let us set before us, as distinctly as we can, the state of an intelligent and thoughtful person who as yet has not heartily received the gospel. He has been led, we will suppose, to some degree of acquaintance with himself, and to some serious reflections on the destiny that may await him.

What, then, are his convictions and feelings? What sort of a self-consciousness has he? What are the obstacles he finds in the way of being satisfied and happy?

He has, first of all, a deep and painful conviction that he is out of his right relations to God and to the universe. He has not, perhaps, very definite apprehensions of the nature and extent of the moral obligations he is under. He does not understand precisely what God would have him be and do. But yet he knows enough to know that the main drift of both his inward and his outward life is wrong; so that he is by no means such a being as he should be. That he wants delight in God; that he lacks the moral qualities which belong to a holy being; that with a strange and humiliating depravity of moral appetite, he is prone continually to what is evil; he is quite distinctly conscious; and all this, he is convinced, should be directly the reverse. He is, therefore, self-condemned. Conscience, whenever he listens to her voice, declares that he is a guilty creature. Of course he also feels that God condemns him, and that justly. The ineffable holiness of the divine character, when he turns his thoughts in that direction, awakens emotions of terror only—none of love—within his heart. If he reads or hears the law of God, and ponders on its import, it is only to perceive that the weight of its condemnation, the terrible wrath which it denounces, rests upon himself; and so, turn where he will, resort to what he will, he has a wearying, crushing burden on his soul.

Along with this, he has the consciousness of moral weakness too. Instead of healthful and tender sensibilities, there is within him the coldness of a death-like apathy. Instead of activity and power to undertake and to perform the right, he seems to himself benumbed and palsied, as it were, and impotent to good. The harmony of his being is all gone; and like a piece of complicated mechanism, whose wheels have lost their original adjustment, and no longer play aright into each other, his moral faculties are all ajar, and will not be combined for the working out of good. His occasional better impulses are overborne by the power of evil. He is in bondage to corruption. It is in vain that he sometimes resolves and makes some struggles to get free. Such efforts come to nothing, and only serve to show him how heavy and how strong the chains that bind him are. He finds, as a fact of fearful omen, that by a law that reigns within him, when he would do good, evil is present with him.

Still further, in addition to all this, he feels deep in his soul desires the most insatiable and restless. With all his efforts he has not been able in the least to appease the sense of inward want. He has often fancied that he was going to do it speedily; but he has always found himself deceived. No pleasures of sense, no gratifications of imagination and of taste, no heights of honour or of power, no treasures of knowledge, no gifts of genius consciously possessed, no affluence and magnificence of wealth; not any, nor all, of the many forms of finite good which surround him on all sides, and of which he has been able to make experiment, or form a judgment, appear when carefully examined at all adapted to satisfy the craving which he feels. He is sure, at last, that they cannot do it. His longings are for something congenial with the highest and the strongest instincts of his spiritual nature. It is something vast, something noble, something infinitely grand and lovely, something holy and divine, and enduring as eternity itself, that he is reaching after. He knows not what it is, nor where, nor how, he is ever going to find it. Yet he perceives that so long as such appetites are burning unsatisfied within his soul, he never can have rest, never can even approximate to a state of happiness. Look where he will, try what he will, his heart yearneth evermore.

Such is a very general, and of course a very imperfect sketch, of the state of an enlightened and seriously reflecting person, who has not as yet received Christ and the gospel to his heart. What with the sense of guilt that haunts him, the want of moral strength and freedom which he feels, and the consciousness of necessities that nothing he has found will satisfy, he has in his own bosom all the ingredients of a hopeless wretchedness—the elements indeed of hell itself. There needs nothing but the steady march of time, as he all too plainly sees, to fill up the measure of his iniquity and his despair.

Now let us, in the second place, suppose that this same person is led, through divine grace, heartily to believe the gospel—to make the actual experiment of its power upon himself. He accepts Christianity as a system really from God. He sees in its provisions a ground of hope for him. He commits his soul to Christ, as the New Testament directs, and believes the promise that through his sacrifice and mediation, he shall be accepted of God, and sanctified and saved. He is now a Christian, in the true and spiritual meaning of the term. He has begun to know, by its influence felt within him, how much efficiency the gospel really has, as a means of relief for necessities like his. What then is the result? What has he found in Christ, and in his word?

He has found, first, pardon and justification. At the sight of Jesus, God's own Son, voluntarily suffering in his stead—bearing his iniquity—dying to redeem him from the curse—he feels that mercy may be shown to him—a sinner, and yet divine justice be untarnished. His own conscience is satisfied. The law of God he perceives is honoured without his punishment. His heart, once cold and hard, is melted now; and he weeps warm, gushing tears of genuine contrition, while he gazes long and tenderly on the great atoning sacrifice. Now the pressure of his conscious guilt is gone. His sins are not forgotten; he never—never can forget them. Nor has he ceased to feel that they are hateful; on the contrary, he loathes them more and more. But they do not make him wretched now. They do not fill his soul with fears. The thunders of the law are hushed. When he ventures to look upward to the holy throne of God, he meets the greeting smile of a Father reconciled, and perceives that he is now acknowledged as a child of the Most High. In short, he is the blessed man whose iniquities are forgiven, whose sin is covered, and to whom there remaineth no more condemnation. He is justified by faith and has peace with God—a consciousness of inward harmony, both with his character and government.

He has found, too, inward grace—the grace of the Holy Ghost—which has now begun to work effectually in that weak, disordered, fettered soul of his, that but a little while before was so powerless in relation to all good. The pulses of new life have begun to beat within his heart. The Spirit that helpeth his infirmities, has so quickened his moral sensibilities, that now they feel the impression of holy objects. The enfeebled powers have received new vigour; and by the healthful stimulus of holy love are urged into activity in the attempt to meet the demands of duty. If there are yet conflicts, many conflicts, in his heart, yet sin no longer reigns there. His enemies give back. The all-sufficient grace of Christ sustains his feebleness, and enables him not only to maintain his ground, but to gain successive victories. In a word, he who before was in a miserable bondage, and could not break his bands, has now begun to taste the freedom of the holy; is fast becoming divested of all his fetters; and in the strength of God, already exults in the prospect of certain and complete deliverance. He feels himself, in this respect, a new creature in Christ Jesus.

Finally, the person whose case we are supposing, in making trial of Christ and of his gospel, has found the inward satisfaction which his craving soul desired. We do not mean to say that his satisfaction is yet perfect. In the earlier stages of his Christian life, the influences of the Christian scheme of grace and truth have only begun to reach and affect his heart; and of course have only answered their end in part. But so much as this is true. This man who just now felt that he had appetites that never yet had found their proper objects; who felt the inexpressible longings of a soul whose profoundest wants were wholly unrelieved; this restless, hungry, thirsty, often baffled and deeply disappointed spirit, has now at last discovered a full supply of the very good he craves. He has found and recognised the bread of life. He has come to the gushing fountain of sweet waters, and at once perceives that this will slake effectually his so long quenchless thirst. He no longer has occasion to weary himself with fruitless searchings. It only now remains that he eat and drink till he is filled and satisfied,—till his soul rests because it has nothing to desire.

Thus, then, the man who before he tried for himself the efficacy of Christianity as a remedy for his distresses, was oppressed with a consciousness of guilt, was held through moral weakness in a grievous vassalage to evil, and was tortured constantly by cravings that could not be appeased; has found, on actually admitting the gospel to his heart, his sense of guilt removed, his shattered nature raised up and disenthralled, and his famishing spirit put in possession of a full supply of congenial and satisfying good. He has received into his soul, with Christ and the gospel, the germs of immortal life and the beginnings of an immortal blessedness. This, he has learned by his own personal experience, is what Christianity can do for a sinful man like him.

With such a case before us as this which we have stated —and this is only the case of ordinary occurrence—we are put in a position to see and feel the force of the experimental argument for the truth and value of the gospel. Here is a man who, when he was guilty, helpless, and pining with inward want, has been induced to make trial of the Christian method of relief. He has come to Christ for help, and thankfully accepted the provisions of his gospel. In doing this he has found effectual deliverance from his miseries; the very deliverance he sought. He has reached the very happiness which his soul instinctively demanded, and which he had ranged creation over, all in vain, to find. There is no mistake in this. He *was* wretched; he *is* at peace. He *was* in galling chains; he *is* in glorious liberty. He *was* perishing of inward hunger; he *is* rejoicing in a satisfaction that is in its nature pure and full, and needs only to be made complete in measure.

And now, suppose you go to him with difficulties; you try to shake his confidence in the divinity of the Christian scheme; you object to the mysteries it involves. You point to its hard sayings. You tell him of the uncertainties of human testimony; of the liability of history, and even of records to corruption; of antagonism between Christian doctrine and the teachings of reason and philosophy; of myths and allegories converted into narratives of facts, and so on to the end of all that you can urge; and what, when you have done? Can you destroy his consciousness? Can you take from him the memory of the past, or change the reality of the present? Can you convince him that he never has experienced what he knows that he *has* experienced as well as he knows that he exists? Will anything constrain him to believe that He was not from heaven, whose word and Spirit have wrought with such heavenly energy upon himself? that that gospel is not from God which has had power to recover his poor wandering soul to holy life and happiness in God, and to fit it to serve and enjoy him even as the angels? No; none of all these things is it possible to do —in the case of one who has really had experience of the effect of the gospel heartily received. Just in proportion to the clearness and certainty of the experience, will be, in each particular case, the strength of the conviction that Jesus is indeed the Son of God, and that in him there is help and hope for all the sinful and the suffering who will take him as their Saviour. You may as well convince the recovering patient, that the balm which has soothed and healed his smarting wounds, is poison; as well persuade a man who was famished, but has eaten and been nourished into strength again, that the food which has refreshed him and satisfied his appetite is innutritious and unwholesome, as bring the thoroughly experimental Christian to conclude that the gospel is not true. It is in this way that we explain the fact—at which unbelief has sometimes sneered—that thousands have lived and died in a tranquil and unfaltering faith, who never read or heard a formal argument for the truth of their religion, and were almost wholly uninstructed in the historic proofs. Let it not be falsely said that they have been believers without evidence—mere dotards, who believed because they were so taught. The furthest possible from this is true. They had the highest kind of evidence on which to rest their faith. Instead of raising questions about the gospel, they put it to the test. They actually *tried* its saving power, and found it mighty to restore their souls; and so they knew it to be divinely true. It was enough for them that it assuaged their inward anguish; that it dried their tears of sorrow; that it gave them life, and power, and freedom, along with the peace of God that passeth understanding; that it stripped death of its chief terrors, and enabled them to see, far over the dark waters, the shining gates and the serene abodes of heaven. They *knew* in whom they had believed.

This, then, you will perceive, is the alternative which is presented to the mind of every person who has so entered into the spirit of Christianity as really to have felt its power; when the question of its truth is agitated, namely, to consent to bear the miseries and wants of which the sinful soul is conscious, unrelieved; or quietly to rest upon the truth of that which gives him the relief he needs, unto the end. Precisely in this way the matter presented itself to the disciples according to the text. **Will ye also go away?** was the question asked to **test** them. Lord, to whom shall we go? was the reply—*Thou* hast the words of eternal life. *Nothing* to be found *away* from Christ—*all* to be found *in* Christ. Who would consent to turn away from blessedness when he has found it, or entertain the idea at all, that that which blesses him supremely is mere falsehood and deceit? A wise man must answer in this manner: Ask me to go away from Christ and disbelieve his words! Go where? I must demand. I cannot go to Paganism. Its systems, even the most ancient and refined of them, have become effete and dead, besides that they are grovelling and mean. I cannot go to Judaism. The vail of its temple has been rent, and it is only a body from which the spirit has departed. I cannot go to Atheism; ah, no, for it crushes the soul's last hope and fills the universe with gloom. I cannot go to Deism; it offers nothing to relieve my conscience, or warm my soul with life. I cannot go even to philosophy, however plausibly and acutely she discourses; she will but freeze my heart amidst her cold abstractions, or leave me hopelessly bewildered in her labyrinths to starve. I cannot go to any creature, nor any finite thing; not even an angel could give me the relief I need, and my desires cry out for something as a good that is infinite and divine. Where, then—oh, tell me *where* I am to go, when I turn my back upon the gospel. In Christ I find just what I cannot do without—eternal life. Why should I let it go? How can I for an instant doubt that He is truth itself who brings me this great gift? He *must* be the true Saviour of the world who *has* delivered me from sin and wrath, has brought me into sympathy and peace with God, and has given me the beginnings of a full and satisfying blessedness. Ah, yes, thou in whom I have found salvation! I *believe* and am *sure*, that thou art that Christ the son of the living God!

It is thus that our holy religion, the faith of Jesus Christ, authenticates itself to those who make a fair experiment of its power. It so meets the entire necessities of the sinful human soul, as to leave nothing more to be desired. Its efficacy is the absolute demonstration of its truth.

It may then easily be seen where those who follow Christ may find the cause of their occasional misgivings—of the questionings and doubts, which, perhaps, in their darker hours, disturb them. If we, who are believers, are sometimes so disturbed; if now and then the mists of uncertainty seem to gather in our spiritual horizon, one of two things, it is obvious, must be true. Either the experience which we have of the effects of the gospel on the soul is very small, or else we have not sufficiently attended to it and reflected on its import. No doubt, with far too many of us the first is the real truth. It is but very poorly that we have tested the power of Christ and of the gospel. We have not entered deeply and earnestly enough into the spirit of the vital and peculiar Christian truths. We have given too little time and thought to the right understanding of their application to ourselves. We have not studied Christ enough; we have not listened to his words enough; and hence our Christian experience lacks depth, and definiteness, and certainty. If this be so, no wonder that the testimony which our experience gives, is faltering. It will only speak out with distinct, and firm, and decisive tones, when our whole hearts are subjected to the influence of the gospel.

But, it may be, that with some the other supposition is the true one. There may be some who have entered deeply into the spirit of Christ and the Christian doctrines, and yet have painful perplexities at times. Objections are urged, perhaps, on grounds of philosophy or history, which they do not know how to answer, and doubts of one sort and another are suggested, which though repelled disturb their peace, while it hardly occurs to them to look within them for the ground of an unfaltering confidence.

If such is the case of any of us who have believed, what we should do is plain. Instead of listening to vain cavils, or even to real difficulties, urged upon us, we have just to stop and seriously consider what has been *wrought in* us—what we ourselves have felt. We have followed Christ. We have gazed upon his glory. We have availed ourselves of his bleeding sacrifice and have come through him to God, and what has the effect been? What has this gospel done for *us?* Ah—now the light breaks on us. We see that nothing but God's own truth can have wrought so mightily, so savingly in us; and we plant our feet, as it were, anew upon the Rock of Ages, and feel it more than ever solid and secure. Let us see to it, that we have a thorough Christian experience, and that we use it to the honour of our Master, as we ought.

Nor can we fail to detect the error involved in the plea

which many urge, that they cannot receive the gospel because they have some speculative objections which have not yet been answered. Men often seem to think that this plea is entirely valid; and yet, if the view which we have taken be a just one, it is altogether futile. For we have seen that the easiest and the surest way to ascertain whether the gospel be divine, is actually to try it, for the restoration and the comfort of our souls. A sick man may have doubts about the power of the remedy which is prescribed. What, then, shall he stop and discuss it at all points? Then he may die before the discussion is gone through. No—he must *take* the remedy at once, and *try* its virtue; and if he feels it easing his keen distress—if he feels the genial glow of health returning through its influence—then his objections are all answered. It is precisely so in relation to the gospel. Shall a man who is ready to die under the burden of his guilt and misery, and who sees that the universe of creatures can give him no relief, refuse to make trial of Christ and of his word till he gets absolute demonstration at all points that Christianity is a divine provision? It ought to be enough that there is reasonable ground of *hope* that Christianity is true, O hesitating child of sin and suffering, to decide you to try its efficacy on you. Without it you are *sure* to sink under the weight of your iniquity into eternal death. You have seen yourself what changes it has wrought in others. You have seen the wretched, when brought to receive it heartily, made to rejoice with a joy that words could not express. You have seen those who have believed transformed in their temper and their lives, and made examples of purity and goodness. So far the experience of others is available, as proof, to you. It is weak, as well as infinitely hazardous, to delay a reception of the gospel for the sake of resolving doubts, when the truth may be known with certainty by coming at once and placing your soul under the full impression of its power.

Ah! you who have stood querying and lingering when you should have fairly and sincerely tried the way of life proposed in Jesus Christ, be persuaded to make the great experiment, while time and opportunity are granted. The witness of thousands and thousands who *have* made it, is given to the truth of the blessed gospel. Martyrs, from out the fires that have burned their bodies into ashes, have testified of its blessed fruits in them; and dying saints, many whom you yourselves have known and loved, who have built their hopes on Christ and his rich promises, have whispered with their pallid lips the words of a full assurance. They have declared, as they went down into the dark waters, that there was an end of all their fears; and their last accents have been those of conscious victory and joy.

But what, on the contrary, has been the testimony, when testimony has been given, of those who have gone from Christ and from his gospel? It has been the expression of bitter disappointment. They have found that all other trusts were vain. Just in the time of their greatest need, they have seen, with the deepest anguish, their reliances all failing them at once; the foundations on which they had rested have dissolved beneath their feet; and their hopes of eternal life have perished. So shall it be with you, if you will follow in their footsteps. Come, then, with your sins and your necessities, and let it be to-day the language of your hearts, To whom, Lord, shall we go, if we turn away from thee? Thou hast the words of eternal life. We believe, and are sure. that thou art the Christ, the Son of the living God.

IX.

Christianity a Religion of Facts.

JOHN iii. 11: *Verily, verily, I say unto thee, we speak that we do know, and testify that we have seen.*

THESE were the words of the great Author of Christianity. He had just explained to Nicodemus the necessity of the new and spiritual birth in order to an admission into his kingdom. That master in Israel, not clearly understanding what he meant, or wishing to draw him into larger discourse on a topic of such interest, queried, as if doubtingly, as to the possibility of what he taught. This gave the divine Teacher occasion to protest, in the most emphatic manner, that in what he delivered to the world he spoke, not as uttering mere opinions, but as testifying to *facts* of which he had personal and perfect knowledge. It was precisely in this particular that he was so incomparably superior, as an instructor of mankind, not only to the doctors of the Jewish synagogue, but to all the philosophers and moralists of the various Gentile schools. They discussed, reasoned, and conjectured. They dealt in subtle speculations, in nice distinctions, in ingenious inferences, in learned and elaborate research. In the end, however, they arrived at very few sure conclusions. It was no rare thing that they contradicted each other, perplexed themselves, and confounded their disciples. Ever learning, as they imagined, they were never able to come to the certain knowledge of the truth.

It was widely different with Christ. Never man spake like this man—was the extorted confession of his enemies. In plain and simple language, and by the help of the most familiar illustrations, he set before men the great essential facts in regard to their moral condition, necessities, and duties; as the faithful and true witness, giving testimony to what he knew as certainties. Appealing to the mighty works which he publicly performed in proof of his divine commission, and declaring himself to be the Lord from heaven, he insisted that he spake what he did know, and testified what he had seen. There is no alternative, therefore, but that we either reject him, in the face of all evidence, as an intentional and base impostor, or else admit, without the smallest qualification, the facts to which he gave such positive and always earnest witness.

Christianity, then, the religion of Jesus Christ, is essentially a religion of facts. It is as an embodiment and presentation of facts positive and certain, that it is addressed to men, and that faith in it is demanded. On this view, as distinctly set forth in the words of Christ which have been quoted, I wish to insist in this discourse.

First in order, it may be needful to illustrate somewhat the meaning of this statement; and all the more because we apprehend that it may strike some persons, even of those who are most familiar with the Scriptures, strangely. A very considerable part of the New Testament is occupied with the statement and discussion of laws and principles, and with the specification and enforcement of particular moral duties; and hence it is doubtless true that many are wont to think of the Christian religion as a system of difficult and abstruse truths, exceedingly numerous and complicated, and many of them, at least, even beyond the comprehension of ordinary minds. This impression, however, is at once widely at variance with the truth, and most pernicious in its influence. It produces often a feeling of discouragement in thoughtful minds, a despair of ever being able to receive the gospel in an intelligible manner, and of course an aversion to the study of the Scriptures.

It is, indeed, to be readily admitted that there are in the New Testament elaborate, profound, and even in some degree obscure discussions, together with a large amount of purely ethical instruction. But it will be seen, if the matter be considered, that this is by no means inconsistent with the statement that Christianity is, as to its substance, distinctively a religion of facts. For the facts themselves, that constitute the pith and moment of the system, may be few and simple and easy of apprehension; while their relations to each other, to universal truth, and to the practical purposes of life, may afford a wide field for inquiry and discussion. It may be true, it is true, we affirm, that the rich doctrinal and ethical discourses which form so large a part of the writings of the apostles, do find their premises in certain cardinal facts which may be very distinctly stated and very clearly understood. Take away these facts and the whole system falls and comes to nothing. In them, therefore, the essence of Christianity does lie; and when we say that it is essentially a religion of facts, we mean to assert that the facts referred to form, so to speak, the staple material, the substance of which it is composed, the ground of its discussions and practical appeals. Assuming some facts as revealed in nature, and discoverable by reason, or written on the heart, it connects with these others before unknown, and many of them beyond the reach of the highest human wisdom. These disclosures of facts unknown, revelations in the strictest sense, are the grand distinction of the Christian Scriptures. It is to these that the Bible, as a whole, owes its peculiar and inestimable value. Their certainty rests on no human discovery, no logical deduction, no insight of reason; but is established by the direct and explicit testimony of God himself, the God of infinite knowledge and absolute veracity.

Here, then, as a second step, we come to the inquiry—What are these facts the assertion of which, with divine authority, is the distinguishing peculiarity of the Christian religion? We ought to be able to set them definitely before us.

Assuming as manifest to reason, and strongly re-asserting the existence, personality, and infinity of God, Christianity declares, as facts, the following things:—

It teaches, as a fact, that God exists eternally as Father, Word, and Spirit; or that there is a trinity in the unity of the Godhead.

It teaches, as a fact, that God administers a perfect and universal government over the worlds of matter and of mind; a government of natural and moral law.

It teaches, as a fact, that, in the universe of mind, benevolent love is the grand harmonizing force, the legitimate result of which is perfection of character and state, or holiness and happiness, in other words; and that selfishness is the great antagonistic and disturbing force, the legitimate result of which is imperfection of character and state, or sin and misery.

It teaches, as a fact, that the whole human race is naturally in a state of moral ruin; having fallen entirely from the state of benevolent love, and into the state of reigning selfishness, and so from happiness to misery as their inevitable ultimate condition, unless deliverance come from without themselves.

It teaches, as a fact, that Jesus of Nazareth was God incarnate, the Word made flesh; and that in his sufferings and death an atonement was made for human sin, which has rendered the exercise of mercy towards repenting sinners consistent with the sense of right in God and man, and with general justice and good government.

It teaches, as a fact, that Christ rose from the dead, and ascended into heaven, where he now lives and reigns as Head of the Christian economy.

It teaches, as a fact, that the Holy Spirit of God is sent to make an effectual application of the atonement, by the renewing and sanctification of those who shall be saved.

It teaches, as a fact, that the resurrection of Christ was a type and pledge of the resurrection of all mankind, and that this sublime event stands immediately connected with a general judgment and eternal retributions of happiness or misery.

It teaches, finally, as a fact, that the gospel is ultimately to reach the whole world with its benefits, and to elevate and bless the entire race on earth in a very high degree.

There are many minor facts which are either necessarily involved in these, or more or less remotely connected with them. But these appear to be the leading cardinal facts to which Christianity gives authoritative witness, and which are the foundation and the substance of what is peculiar in the system. Considering how vast the reach and moment of the scheme, they are wonderfully few and simple. They are stated with great distinctness, may be clearly understood, and readily remembered. They *are* mere *facts*, affirmed in plain statements of what actually is. They are not problems submitted to reason for solution. They are not *dogmas* as they are sometimes a little contemptuously called. There has been, no doubt, an abundance of dogmatism in the discussions held as to the significance and the relations of these facts; and many dogmas of human origin, miserable and worthless, have sometimes been connected with them in the multifarious discussions of the schools. But we should always carefully discriminate between the clearly stated facts of divine revelation and all the reasonings and philosophies about them. The former will remain unchanged though the latter be scattered to the winds.

In nature, we well know, there are certain facts which are obvious and not to be disputed; such as relate, for example, to attraction, light, heat, organization, animal and vegetable life, and a thousand other things. These facts are the essential things in the natural world; the basis of all true knowledge, and of all sound philosophy in reference to such matters. They lie at the foundation of all reasoning and judgment in the practical affairs of life, and are the ground of all wise action. They are the *realities* of nature.

Just so the facts to which we have alluded as being anthoritatively taught in the Christian system, are the realities of the moral and spiritual world; some of them partially discoverable by reason, all of them known perfectly by God, and by him explicitly revealed. We speak that we do know, says Christ, and testify that we have seen. By the testimony of the senses we learn the facts of the material universe. By the testimony of God himself we learn the facts of the spiritual and moral universe.

The latter are not less certain than the former; nor is the knowledge of them less necessary to the real welfare of mankind. Those persons who, with an air of superior wisdom, decry the Christian doctrines, that is to say, the great facts of Christianity, as of very little consequence as regards a Christian life, exhibit precisely the same stupidity as if they should assert that, as regards our natural life, the facts and laws of nature are of little or no importance. Were it not so common an occurrence, it would seem incredible that any intelligent person could give utterance to so shallow and absurd a sentiment.

It is, in truth, only when Christianity is regarded as an authoritative setting forth of the most material facts in the moral world, that its admirable adaptation to the wants of all mankind can be appreciated fully. Let this be carefully considered. No system of abstruse doctrines, of subtle and nicely elaborated philosophy, or of truths recondite in their nature, or resting on proofs remote and difficult of apprehension, could ever be applicable to men of all conditions throughout the world. Views and opinions which one individual, or one people, might be able to understand and to receive, might be entirely unsuited to the genius, the culture, or the capabilities of another. There are such wide diversities among mankind in these respects, that to human wisdom, the idea of giving a religious system which should be equally adapted to the barbarous and the civilized, the ignorant and the learned, the weak in intellect and the strong in intellect, would probably have seemed, beforehand, entirely impracticable, if not absurd.

But God is wiser than men. It is one of the decisive marks of its divine origin which the Christian religion carries with it, that it is a complete realization of this very idea of availability for all. Wonderful as it is in the grandeur and interest of its disclosures, vast as are the regions of thought which it opens or suggests, and mighty as its influence is seen to be wherever it is heartily received, a few distinctly stated facts, as we have seen, make up the sum and substance of what is peculiar to the system. But simple facts all men can apprehend and feel, if not with the same facility, and to precisely the same extent, yet so as to experience their practical effects on the character and life. It has been found by actual experiment that the Hottentot, the Greenlander, the

Esquimaux, and the savage dweller in the islands of the sea, not less than the most intellectual and polished people of the world, accept the religion of the cross, exemplify its power to elevate and bless, and living and dying enjoy its blessed consolations. Its facts in regard to God and providence, to sin, the Saviour, the future life and the retributions of eternity, and others allied to these, when taken as they stand in the Holy Scriptures, aside from human reasonings, in their true simplicity and naked force, gain easy access to the mind when once it is drawn to give them a serious attention. No great enlargement of the intellect, no high degree of learning, nor any peculiarity of culture is required for their reception. As the whole race. notwithstanding all diversities, have certain great wants in common, so it is found that to meet and satisfy these wants, the facts of the Christian revelation, to which He who spake what he did know has testified, have a common applicability. They avail for all alike. Christianity is, in this view, admirably fitted to become the religion of the world.

Since, then, Christianity, as a divine religion, is fundamentally a revelation of the great moral and spiritual facts to which we have referred—facts by which especially it is fitted to reach the whole human race—a third inquiry will naturally suggest itself. How ought such a religious system to be treated? In what state of mind should we approach it? How give it its best practical effect?

On this point we may first observe that its clearly stated facts are always and distinctly to be recognised as such. It is for want of attention to this obvious dictate of sound reason, that many who seem to be sincere inquirers are tossed perpetually on the restless sea of doubt. They confound known facts with speculative conjectures and opinions. Instead of seizing and holding what is certain they forget that *any* thing is certain. They suffer themselves to be drawn away from what is tangible and real into the shadowy realm of the unknown, and so are led to waste their time and strength, their thought and feeling, in raising and discussing questions which end in nothing after all. The plain facts which Christianity embodies and affirms are not now to be debated. They rest already on the highest possible evidence, and no longer require to be established. We may profitably, we must, to some extent, inquire into the relation and the bearings of these facts; but unless we are willing to involve ourselves in hopeless difficulties, we are to accept them as the well determined realities which they actually are.

Suppose a man, in a spirit of captious scepticism, refuses to admit the obvious facts of nature, which are every day before his eyes; and as some misnamed philosophers have done, sets himself to doubt the testimony of his senses, and, as it were, to tear up the very foundations of all knowledge. At what results would he be likely to arrive? You would expect to see him every moment more and more entangled and bewildered, and would hardly count him worthy to be reckoned in the number of sane men. To spend one's time in making it a question whether the sun shines, or the grass grows, or bodies attract each other, or in trying to raise doubts about any other well-known facts in nature, you would certainly regard as a proof of anything but a sound condition of the intellect

Just so it is in regard to the main facts of Christianity —facts which the Son of God appeared on earth to settle finally. Not to assume them as settled, in all our thoughts and reasonings, is to fall into the folly of doubting certainties, ascertained and known to be such. Whether our race be in a fallen state, whether the justice of God condemns us, whether Christ has made atonement for our sins, whether eternal life or death is suspended on our repentance and faith in him, whether Christ has risen, and whether we shall rise to be acquitted or condemned at the bar of a final judgment—are things no more to be debated as if questionable now, than whether a stone will fall to the earth if it be thrown into the air. That they are questioned and debated still by many, is no proof that they are not established facts; it proves simply that those who will not accept them as such are so far blinded and misled through prejudice, or the want of information, that they have no right discernment in the matter. Quite recently a man announced, over his own name, in the public papers, that the received system of astronomy was altogether false, and that he was prepared to show this to the satisfaction of all who would give him their attention. What then? The public, instead of being led to doubt whether the *sun* were the centre of the solar system, were rather led to conclude at once that the *man* had lost his wits. So they who at this day seek to bring into doubt the facts which Christianity unambiguously sets forth, do most of all bring into doubt their own intellectual sobriety and force. Since the Christian revelation was, at the outset, proved to be divine, and has stood impregnable against the assaults of persecuting power, of wit and ridicule, of learning, criticism, and philosophy, its clearly stated facts are justly to be taken as verities for ever settled beyond rational debate; and all systems, all theories, all speculations, and all pretended facts, which are really incompatible with these, may be at once rejected. Nor is there anything of dogmatism or bigotry in this. It is simply refusing to surrender what we know to the unreasonable demands of ignorance and perverseness.

It may be added further, secondly, that as a religion of facts, Christianity must be regarded as immutable in its essence, and must be accepted precisely as it is. It has been by no means an uncommon thing to see men, not avowing unbelief, commit the folly of undertaking to correct and modify the Christian revelation; endeavouring to prevent its saying something which it explicitly affirms, or to constrain it to say something which, in truth, it nowhere teaches. Such persons not rarely delude themselves and others. They work out monstrous compounds of truth and error mingled in various proportions—a few grains perhaps, of the divine to many grains of the purely human,—and fancy themselves improvers of Christianity, and wiser than its Author.

But what is the result? With all their ingenuity and pains, they cannot alter the facts which Christianity makes known. What earnest and persevering efforts have been made through centuries, by those who have flattered themselves that they were profound thinkers and philosophers, to make the Christian system different in something from what it really is! How vast the amount of time and labour expended in this manner, and all how utterly in vain! The same great facts remain to which the divine teacher testified when he spake what he positively knew and bear witness to what he had actually seen; and so they will remain for ever! They are like old, grey rocky mountains, which stand unharmed through the beating storms of ages. The cunning inventions of human wisdom, opinions and philosophies in perpetual succession, encounter them, as clouds encounter the hoary cliffs, only to be themselves dissolved and scattered to the winds, and to leave them just what they were before. You may try, O men of speculation, to change, in the natural world, the fact of magnetic attraction or of the gravitating force; but the body will still fall and the needle will still be steady to the pole. Even so when you shall have done your utmost to change the essential facts of the Christian revelation, you will leave them as you find them—the unalterable realities of the moral universe of God. It is a noble characteristic of our divine religion that as to its substance and ground, it is immutable and permanent. It must be accepted as it is, or rejected altogether. The attempt to modify it is forbidden by sound reason and sound piety alike.

Still further, thirdly, it is plain that in order to give Christianity its proper influence and power upon the world, its distinctive facts must be continually insisted on. There are two opposite errors which have at times prevailed in relation to this matter. It has sometimes been the case that the Christian ministry and Church have fallen into a scholastic and speculative habit. They have at least seemed to regard the facts of revealed religion, not so much in their practical applications in their bearing on the character and welfare, the hopes and destinies of men, as in the light of interesting objects of thought and study, to be arranged, and classified, and constructed into systems, as specimens of birds or minerals are studied, prepared and labelled, and set in the cases of a cabinet. Treated in such a manner, the solemn, stirring, and vital facts, or doctrines as they are quite as often called, of the Christian faith, become indeed mere *dogmas*, in the offensive meaning of the term—dry, abstract, and comparatively inoperative dogmas. They lose their power to stimulate and rouse the soul, and do but little more than entertain the understanding. From such an exhibition of Christianity but little life or motion will be likely to result.

But one extreme is apt to beget another. Reacting from this excessively and drily dogmatic form of Christian teaching, there are some who would have little or nothing definitely said about the essential facts of revelation. They wish to have the teachers of religion leave off insisting on the fact of human guilt, the fact of a redemption by the cross, the fact of a needed spiritual renovation, and so on to the end; and they would have them give themselves almost entirely to the inculcation of what is purely ethical—to the work of exhorting men to the outward duties which Christianity imposes. Instead of labouring to have the system intelligently comprehended and felt in its full energy within the soul, there to become a source and fountain of right action of all sorts, they think it better to insist almost exclusively on action, and to leave the gaining of right knowledge and the kindling of right feeling in the soul—which things alone give moral power—to be accomplished as they may.

It is hard, perhaps, to say which of these errors is the worse. The one converts what should be quick and powerful into something nearly or quite inert and useless. The other changes what should be spiritual, earnest, and profound, into something which is chiefly formal and outward, a heartless and superficial semblance of zeal for what is good, and not the thing itself. Give over insisting on the great facts which the New Testament asserts, and confine yourself to the teaching of mere ethics, and in a single generation Christianity ceases to be known in its peculiar features. Let such a course be universal, and it must soon become extinct. It is the constant reiteration of the momentous facts of the holy gospel, the clear and forcible exhibition of them in their certainty and their vast solemnity and interest, that causes them to become inwrought into the minds of those who hear them, and especially of the young, who in fresh crowds are all the while advancing into life. It is in this way that Christian knowledge as related to character and life is perpetuated and made effectual to its end.

In order, therefore, to the progress of Christianity and

to the right application of it for the saving of men's souls and the curing of the evils that afflict a sinful world, its facts must be forcibly presented and pressed on the attention of all who can be reached. There must be special care to exhibit them in their own simplicity, in their direct relation to practicl duty of all kinds, in a word, in their bearing on the actual condition and necessities of men. When so set forth and urged, the facts of our religion, or doctrines as they are with equal fitness called, exert a mighty power upon hearts prepared by the divine spirit to receive them. They furnish to each individual soul the reasons, grounds, and motives of right action—the impulses which prompt it to strive with all earnestness to meet the demands of duty, and to do good to the extent of its ability.

It only remains to be added, that since Christianity is a religion of facts, of positive realities, the obligation of every individual heartily and practically to receive it, must be allowed to be imperative and not to be escaped. No one in his senses can hesitate to acknowledge that he is bound to act in accordance with the great facts of the natural world, in the ordering of his natural life; and that he must expect to suffer, and will deserve to suffer, the greatest calamities if foolishly he should refuse to do so. How then can it be doubted, that I, that you, and others, are bound to act in accordance with the great facts of the spiritual world in the ordering of our spiritual life; and that to refuse to do it is to involve ourselves in miseries beyond endurance. It often seems as if those who hear the gospel, and in a general sense admit its claims, were resting after all in the false idea that Christianity is very much a religion of opinions, and that it cannot be very material whether they personally adopt these opinions or neglect them. They feel, apparently, that they are at liberty to think and act very much as it may suit them in regard to the disclosures of divine revelation, provided they do not directly array themselves against them.

No, no; this is a great and dangerous delusion. God, the soul, guilt, redemption, the resurrection from death, and eternal joy or woe—these are, as we have seen, facts positively determined by Christianity—by the gospel of Jesus Christ as found in the New Testament. Suppose you refuse them your assent, or even your particular attention; suppose in your heedlessness you quite forget them;—it is all the same. You will find them realities at last. Suppose you admit, and really believe them intellectually, and only disregard them practically, perhaps with a serious purpose to regard them soon or late. It will still remain that they are facts—facts touching your duty and your happiness at every point. You may live and die neglecting them, and go at last, as ruined souls, to a lost eternity; but they will be facts for ever! It will for ever be true that they had such relation to all the interests of your being, that you were bound, by the highest conceivable obligations, to heed them in the moulding of your characters and the shaping of your ends.

Remember this, I pray you—that in this divine religion, which, in the name of God, is pressed on your attention, you have to do with facts from which there is no escape. Admit them, act as they demand, build on them, as on an adamantine basis, the structure of your character and hopes, and it shall be to the exaltation, peace, and glory of the immortal future that awaits you. Pursue an opposite course, and you will surely verify at last, in your own melancholy experience, the fearful words of Christ: "Whosoever falleth on this stone shall be broken; but on whomsoever *it shall fall it shall grind him to powder!*"

X.

Mystery no Obstacle to Faith.

1 Cor. ii. 7: *But we speak the wisdom of God in a mystery.*

EACH human being at his birth has everything to learn. We bring into being with us the faculties which fit us to become intelligent,—a mental constitution from which perceptions, intellectual processes and ideas, in proper time and by the natural course of things, result. As we are brought in contact with external objects, the mind is awakened into consciousness; its elementary laws of thought reveal themselves; and thenceforward it goes on, more or less rapidly, in the acquisition of positive knowledge.

The child, when the sense of his own ignorance and a desire to learn have been awakened in his heart, is apt to imagine that those who are older than himself, and whom he has found able to answer his first inquiries, know almost everything. He believes that when he too shall become a man, he shall, in like manner, clearly comprehend those things at which now he can only wonder. As he advances to maturer years, therefore, and new subjects of interest continually present themselves, he goes on asking others to explain; and he is surprised and disappointed when he finds, in many instances, that no sufficient explanation, and no solution of his difficulties, can be given. He finds it hard to relinquish the idea of having everything made entirely plain to his understanding; and under the influence of this reluctance, he is inclined to doubt or disbelieve whatever is inexplicable—whatever, in other words, offers itself as a mystery to his mind.

In this vulnerable point, scepticism in reference to subjects of a religious nature is wont to assail the mind. It exaggerates the mysteriousness of the facts and doctrines of religion—of revealed religion more especially—and affects to regard it as something strange that these should be attended with difficulties, and should some of them seem so much beyond the reach of the natural understanding. It would have it believed that obscurity—mystery—is something *peculiar* to religion, and not to be found in other departments of our knowledge, and then insists that what is so incomprehensible cannot rationally be believed. By this specious, but unsound and fallacious style of argument, the faith of many has, without doubt, been overthrown.

We say that the argument against revealed religion drawn from the mysteries involved in some of its truths, is not valid. It is neither true, as it assumes, that mystery pertains only, or at least pre-eminently, to matters of religion; nor that nothing that includes impenetrable mysteries can be entitled to belief. We purpose, on the contrary, now to show that mystery pertains to all other things which we believe as truly as to the doctrines of divine revelation; and that if we cannot receive anything mysterious as truth, then we cannot receive as truth anything at all. One course of argument and illustration will establish both these points.

That there are unfathomable mysteries involved in revealed religion is readily conceded. The apostle boldly avows it in the text: "We speak," says he, "the wisdom of God in a mystery." The being of God, the foundation of all religion, is itself a mystery. We can form no conception of his essence. The mind sinks exhausted in the effort to take in the eternity of his duration, or the infinity of his power. His self-existence is an abyss that swallows up our thoughts. When in our efforts to conceive him as he is, we have combined our highest notions of wisdom, of power, of justice, of goodness, and of the morally beautiful and sublime, we have fallen as far below the great reality, as does the infant when pleased with the splendour of the sun, of a just comprehension of the mechanism of the universe. The providence of God, which revelation represents as universal, is a mystery. That he should sustain the universe and fill it with his presence, at every moment bringing myriads of creatures into being, displaying everywhere the most admirable workmanship, controlling all things by his will, never reposing for an instant in the midst of his infinite affairs, and yet fainting not, neither becoming weary—all this it is utterly impossible for us with finite powers to comprehend. The system of redemption, through which, according to the gospel, God offers eternal life to sinful men, dating its origin in the deep counsels of eternity, unfolding the divine mercy in its immeasureable riches, involving the wonderful fact of the incarnation of the Word and the mission and inscrutable ministry of the Spirit, is equally a mystery acknowledged. So is the truth of the trinity in the unity of God. So is spiritual existence, and the resurrection of the body to immortal life. All these, and many other truths which are essential parts in the scheme of revealed religion, are confessedly mysterious. But when the plea is urged that they are in this respect peculiar, and that it is unreasonable and extraordinary that we should be required to believe things so mysterious in themselves, or their relations, we at once join issue on the point and deny that there is anything peculiar in the case, or anything contrary to reason in the requirement; and we assert, on the contrary, as already stated, that there is in fact mystery in everything, and that this proves, in a multitude of cases, no obstacle at all to the most firm belief.

Let us look at a few facts. Of nothing can we feel a greater certainty than of our own being and personal identity. No imaginable evidence can add to the strength of my conviction that I exist, and that I am the same individual being that I was twenty years ago. But *what* am I? I can no more understand the essence of my conscious self, than I can that of God the Infinite Spirit. The intellectual activities—

"These thoughts that wander through Eternity"—

that flash with a speed that outstrips the lightning across the universe, that travel from world to world, and ascend from the insect to the Deity without effort or fatigue,—what know I of their nature? Or where is he that can resolve my doubts and tell me what they are? These sensibilities that make me capable of so many and such various affections by contact with things without me, capable of being moved to admiration by the view of beauty, to awe at the sight of the sublime, to love in the contemplation of the pure and good; what can I tell, or what can I learn of their hidden constitution? The philosopher here is no wiser than the child. That wonderful faculty, the will, by what means can I draw aside the veil that conceals its operations? It acts unseen within me as the helmsman of my destiny, turning me hither and thither, and commanding every power by its simple act of choice. The material body, in all its members and nearly all its functions, obeys its secret energy. It is the attribute, finally, which makes me moral and responsible. Yet I know as much of the structure of the furthest world in space as I know of its essential nature. My own being is a mystery.

Then, further, as to my personal identity—what is it precisely that constitutes me the same individual that I was at any moment past? My body is not composed of the same matter; perhaps not one of the same particles are in it now which at some former period it contained. Yet it is the same body and not another. My mind, too, has been perpetually passing through changes of thought, feeling, and affection. Its opinions, tastes, desires, are widely different from what they were in other years. Yet after all, it is the same and not another mind. Its thread of conscious identity has not been broken and never will be broken. How inscrutable a mystery is this!

Turn then, if you please, to nature in any of her various

departments. Look, for instance, at the facts presented in the animal kingdom. Explain, if you can, the nature of that something to which you have given the name of instinct. Observe that spider, which has spread her gossamer across your window. How did she learn to construct that octagon, as perfect as if drawn by the nicest geometrician? Or watch the robin that has fixed her nest on the tree that shades your door. That nest is the first she ever built; yet see how perfect—the most practised of her kind has never formed a better. Where did she gain her skill in architecture? Note too with what self-denying perseverance she sits upon her eggs; it is her first time of incubation. How came she to know that such an act was necessary, and that her long patience will be at length rewarded?

Consider also animal life itself, and the functions of the vital economy. What is it that prevents the decomposition of the flesh of animals so long as the vital principle is there, while decay commences the moment it is gone? Lay open the mode of the assimilating process, and tell us how it is that the gross substances taken in the form of food are converted into the beautiful carnation of the human cheek, and the gorgeous and variegated dyes of birds and insects. Show what it is that keeps the heart for ever throbbing, and the lungs perpetually heaving, without any effort of the will. Solve the long doubts of the philosophers, and tell us what is the condition of the mind in sleep, and of what stuff dreams are made. You encounter mystery at every step.

Or look again at the vegetable world. There is the rose

blushing crimson by your window. What elements have been concerned in its production? Light, heat, moisture, and the common earth. But by what means have the soft and tender petal, the exquisitely grateful odour, and the hues unrivalled in their loveliness, been elaborated from such materials? How has the same sap been made to produce the hard stalk, the sharp thorn, the green leaf, and the admirable flower? There, too, is the lily by its side. It springs from the same soil, is warmed by the same sun, watered by the same showers, yet instead of having the same colour it is white as the virgin snow. Again, there is the grass and the violet that both spring from one common mould, and yet, one is a soft and lively green, and the other an imperial purple. Once more, you have a seed. It is only a mite in size, but just visible to the unassisted eye, and might easily be mistaken for a particle of dust. Yet, in it lies concealed the germ of a noble plant; and let it be cast into the earth, and it will send forth life and beauty from its own decay, and thus will perpetuate its kind. How unsearchable are all these mysteries!

If now from organized we pass to inorganic matter, the same combination of the known with the unknown meets us. You have here the laws of chemical affinity and repulsion. You find that certain substances when reduced to a fluid state and then placed in given conditions, return to solids by the process of crystallization; and that in doing this one always takes the cubic form, another always that of an octahedron, another always that of a parallelopiped, and so on. But of these, and a multitude of other plain and unquestionable facts, you cannot by the nicest observation detect the cause, or the mode of its operation. Nature veils it in deep mystery.

Lastly, not to prolong our illustration, think of those subtle yet efficient agents that produce the more general and grand phenomena of nature. Put an end to the conjectures of mankind, by telling us what light, and heat, and electricity, and magnetism are. That mighty universal force, to which, by way of concealing our ignorance, we give the name of *gravity;* which brings the pebble to the earth, and chain revolving worlds about their centres; search out the secret and instruct us in relation to its nature. You cannot answer our inquiries. These are nature's hidden things. She wraps them in mystery into which you pry in vain.

You see, then, that mystery is written all over the universe of God. You cannot turn where it is not. You find it in yourself, you perceive it in every creature that hath breath. You see it in every blade of grass, and every flower that beautifies the earth; in every gem that comes from the productive mine; in the radiance of the sun, the gleam of the lightning, in the needle steady to the pole, in the alternations of day and night, the changing of the seasons, and the mechanism of the heavens. There is nothing so familiar, nothing even so trifling around you, that it may not suggest a variety of questions which it is beyond your power to answer.

It is, therefore, manifestly true that we do in reality believe a multitude of facts on the testimony of our senses, and on other evidence, in which the deepest mysteries are obviously involved; thus showing, undeniably that mysteries present no obstacle to the belief of facts or truths supported by a reasonable amount of proof; or, which is saying the same thing, that the certainty of what we know, is not in the least diminished by the uncertainty which may exist in regard to the relations of our knowledge.

Having thus shown the groundlessness of the allegation of the sceptic that things involving mystery are not to be believed, we will now go further still. We will take the full benefit of the argument, by turning the fact that many of the truths of revealed religion are confessedly mysterious, to the confirmation of its divinity. We say, then, that if a system of religion were presented, which professed to be from God, and yet did claim to have no mysteries, this claim itself should prove the system to be false. For such a system would be exceptional and anomalous in our experience; and we should justly reason that if earthly things are found to be beyond our comprehension, much more ought heavenly things to be expected to be so; that if there are mysteries in ourselves and in all the animal creation, in every blade of grass and every flower, in the pebbles beneath our feet, in the clouds above our heads, and in the laws that govern matter; much more ought we to look for them in God, in his vast plan of moral government, in his eternal providence, in the spiritual relations of the human soul, in the means of its recovery from sin, and the determination of its character and destinies for the immortality that lies on the other side of death. When, therefore, the truly enlarged and discerning mind finds that revealed religion, instead of making loud pretensions to simplicity, and claiming to make the infinite perfectly intelligible to the finite, exhibits the grand facts and doctrines of which it treats in the sublimity of their real light and shade, explaining what we have need to know and are now capable of knowing, and leaving other things enwrapped in darkness; it sees, in this, at once, the evidence of honesty and truth, and a conformity to the familiar system of material nature. To such a mind, the mysteries of religion, so far from being obstacles, are positive aids to faith. To the Omniscient only are there no dark and hidden things. A mystery, let it be borne in mind, is not an absurdity—a something at which reason itself revolts—it is simply something not yet understood. Since our capacities are limited, and our power of comprehending the spiritual is particularly feeble, it is, in the nature of the case, impossible, that even by any conceivable revelations, God should bring down to the level of our minds all those truths that lie embosomed in the invisible, the infinite, and the eternal. The whole scheme of revealed religion to him is wisdom, though to us it is delivered, of necessity, in a mystery.

We would not, indeed, assert that God has actually gone to the utmost limit of the possible, in giving a revelation. There is no reason to suppose that he has done this in relation to all subjects, while we may well believe that he has with respect to some. There may be many other reasons, it is plain, besides that of our want of capacity to comprehend him, to render it fit that he should withhold from us many kinds and degrees of knowledge which might without difficulty be imparted. Of such reasons there are some that readily suggest themselves. It might, for example, instead of relieving, only bewilder and perplex us, to have our minds excited to yet higher inquiry by further disclosures as to things that have no immediate relation to our duty or our happiness for the present. Life is so short, so full of engrossing occupation, we are under the necessity of devoting so much of it to what is directly practical, that very little time is allowed us for merely speculative thought. To open too many vistas to our minds, too many and too distant glimpses out into the great universe of things, might only divert our attention from matters of pressing moment, or make these seem to us to be trivial and irksome. Then, further, it is no less obvious that this living in the midst of mysteries may prove a most salutary moral discipline. By contact with the as yet unopened secrets of the universe, our pride receives a salutary check. We find that with all our aspirations and our conscious power of intellect and will, we cannot pass beyond a certain boundary which God has fixed. We are taught to recognise the unimaginable grandeur and glory of that great Being to whose all-embracing mind and all-discerning vision nothing is in any respect obscure. All this is eminently favourable to a right estimate of ourselves and to a just view of our position. The lesson of our ignorance and of the imperfection of our highest faculties as instruments of knowledge, enforced as it is perpetually by the facts of our experience, is well adapted to repress conceit and to beget a reverential spirit. Both as regards the ends of practical life and the development in our souls of sentiments of humility, of veneration, and of worship, there are great advantages to be derived from the present withholding of many parts of divine knowledge which might possibly be revealed. Instead of being impeached, therefore, because of mysteries which might have been made clear, the wisdom and goodness of God find in these very mysteries an impressive illustration. Instead of being an objection to a revelation that claims to be from him, that many of its lines of truth run off into the infinite unknown, we ought to recognise in this fact one of the most distinctive marks of its divine original. The absence of mystery would demonstrate it to be only a shallow cheat.

Instead, then, of suffering ourselves to be perplexed and stumbled because we encounter mysteries in the Christian revelation, it is much wiser, as well as more becoming, certainly, that we cultivate a humble, docile spirit. How exceedingly limited, at best, is our horizon! What an infant, in a sober view, does the wisest man on earth appear, on the scale of universal being! We walk as if by moonlight. We are able to see the form and outline of the things immediately about us, with tolerable distinctness; but of the more remote, we can perceive only the dim shadows. It little befits our state and powers to be self-confident and wise in our own eyes. It is much more suitable to both, that we should take the attitude of children; and that, with a profound willingness to be taught, we should ask of God, the Fountain of eternal wisdom, that he will illuminate our souls and guide us into truth.

We ought likewise to consider, for the enkindling of a

heartfelt gratitude, that the mysteries of our being had been far deeper and darker than they are, but for the partial light which God has afforded in his word. We assume, at this stage of our progress, that the Christian revelation is divine. By the help of this, where the wisest heathen, in all ages, have groped their way, we are able to see distinctly; and though we are able to know so little in comparison with the grand total of truth as open to the infinite mind, yet let us devotedly praise God that he has enabled us to know so much. It is enough to break the gloom of these our mortal days of darkness. It is enough to enable us to discern and keep the path of duty and of life. What though it does not enable us to look, with perfect vision, into the unfathomable depths of glory in the being and the counsels of the Deity, or to solve to our thought the perplexing enigmas of the universe. It ought not only to satisfy us, but to fill our souls with thankfulness, that the light we have is sufficient to lead us to the knowledge of all that is now essential to our welfare.

For the rest, it may content us that we can confidently anticipate the future increase of our knowledge. You are perhaps sometimes impatient now of the limits set to your inquiries. Your restless spirits, as it were, beat against the bars that shut them in, and long to penetrate beyond them and put an end to doubt. Receive, then, with a meek, and penitent, and trusting heart the blessed gospel of the Son of God, and mould by it your temper and your life, and you shall ere long rise to a higher region of existence. There the mysteries that now perplex you will probably most of them be solved. The shadows of earth will no longer lie upon the fields of truth. I do not say that new mysteries will not be found. On the contrary, since you are finite and God is infinite, you must for ever find them. But in the more perfect vision of that brighter world, you will be ever learning; and as old mysteries, one by one, are understood and new ones are presented, your circle of knowledge will be evermore enlarging, and you will find an inexhaustible delight in studying into the secrets of the universe. While, therefore, you are humbled at your ignorance, and grateful for the degree of light you have, submit patiently to mysteries, and await in faith and hope the disclosures of the coming world.

> "Mortal, who with a trembling, longing heart,
> Watchest in silence the few rays that steal
> In their kind dimness to thy feeble sight;
> Watch on in silence—till within thy soul,
> Springs the hid fountain of immortal life
> Then shall the mighty veil asunder rend
> And o'er the spirit living, strong and pure,
> Shall the full glories of the Godhead flow!"

XI.

The Highest Evidence may not Produce Belief.

JOHN xii. 37: *But though He had done so many miracles before them, yet they believed not on him.*

THAT the public ministry of our blessed Lord was altogether extraordinary in its character, even the most determined and malignant of his enemies never pretended to deny. In tone and spirit, in matter and manner, in word and work, it was unlike anything the world had ever known. It was because it was so unique, so original, so striking, that it arrested attention as it did; that it commended itself so powerfully to the candid and sincere, who waited for the consolation of Israel; and excited such implacable hostility in the minds of the proud, the self-righteous, and the sensual.

But while the ministry of Christ had a character so marked that it could not fail to produce a marked impression, its chief value, after all, was to depend on its being unhesitatingly accepted as divine. The grand question to be settled by all who might take an interest in the matter, was,—Is it a ministry which God has instituted, and has distinctly endorsed and ratified, as invested with authority from Him? That such was the fact, it was necessary to have established in the most conclusive manner.

Of course, there was need that the claims of Jesus to have come down from heaven as the Lord's Christ, as God's special ambassador to men, and to have received from the Father the authority which, in his ministry, he assumed and exercised, should be sustained by proofs as extraordinary as the claims themselves. Such proofs, it is alleged, were amply furnished, especially in the astonishing miracles which he wrought in the most public manner, in a great variety of circumstances, and throughout the whole period of his public life. Yet what was the result? The text announces it: "But though he had done so many miracles before them, yet they believed not on him." It strikes us as a *strange* result. The phenomenon is worthy to be studied. By a careful examination of the case we shall be led to some interesting and highly practical conclusions.

How is it to be accounted for, that with all the miracles which he performed before them, so many nevertheless refused to believe in Christ? This question will sufficiently indicate the drift of the remarks which we propose.

We say then, first, that their persistent unbelief did not originate in any doubt as to the reality of the miracles themselves. Of this we are absolutely sure; because the reality of these mighty works was fully admitted by the fiercest of Christ's opposers. That he actually did the things which he seemed to do, without any illusion or collusion in the matter, was habitually acknowledged;

was never, in fact, so far as there is evidence, denied in one solitary instance. They were wrought on all sorts of occasions, among all sorts of people, in the most open manner possible, and with every attending circumstance that could produce conviction; and it was doubtless because they were undeniable, and for no other reason, that they were undenied. It was without the least hesitation that Christ himself appealed to them as the decisive credentials of his divine commission, which he could not have done, had not their reality been universally conceded.

When, for example, John sent to him two of his disciples, demanding, "Art thou he that should come, or do we look for another?" Jesus answered and said unto them, "Go and show John again those things which ye do hear and see. The blind receive their sight, and the lame walk, the lepers are cleansed, the deaf hear, and the dead are raised up." The whole force of this reply lies in the fact that they themselves had witnessed all these things, or most of them at least, which Luke tells us was the case, and that no doubt was thrown upon them from any quarter.

The truth obviously is that very many of the miracles which Jesus did were established by such a kind of proof, and such an amount of proof, that there was not the smallest chance for cavil. When in the crowded street he stopped the funeral procession, and restored the widow's son to life, who of that astonished throng would have ventured to deny the deed? When he multiplied the bread, and fed the five thousand with five loaves, and on another occasion the four thousand with the seven loaves, who of all the multitudes that had themselves both witnessed the wonder and tasted of the food, could have ever questioned that a stupendous miracle was wrought? So as to the opening of the eyes of the man born blind, well known, not only to his parents, but to great numbers who had been acquainted with him from his birth, or had often seen him as he sat begging by the wayside; it was impossible to gainsay the fact when he was seen with his sight restored. So in other cases; particularly in that of Lazarus. That Christ had raised him from the dead, there was no possibility of denying; it was known and acknowledged at Jerusalem, by friends and foes alike.

When, therefore, the Scribes and Pharisees, and those who acted with them, rejected Jesus of Nazareth with all his wondrous works before them, we know that it was not because there was any suspicion as to the miracles themselves. It was impossible for them to do otherwise than own that these miracles were real; and painful as the confession was, they were compelled to make it.

Nor, in the second place, can the unbelief to which the text refers, have originated in any want of adaptation in miracles to produce a conviction of Christ's divine commission.

Although our Lord himself distinctly appealed to his miracles as affording unanswerable proof that he came from God, and although the apostles did the same, and the ablest Christian writers of all ages have agreed in so regarding them, it has become quite the fashion with a certain class of writers in our day to deny that miracles, admitting them as really performed, can establish any truth at all. In support of their position these modern sages insist that no miracle, however great, can supply the several steps in the logical process by which an abstract truth is made clear to the understanding; can give, in other words, a complete demonstration of a theorem. But this assertion is, in reality, nothing to the purpose. The question is not a question of abstract truth at all; but of truth in the concrete—a simple question of fact. A person claims to possess divine power. Does he really possess it?—That is the question. If he performs a miracle he *exercises* divine power. Does not that prove that he possesses it? If a work of God is manifestly wrought, what other demonstration can be asked that the power of God is there?

Besides—although it be admitted that a miracle cannot convey the logical process by which the reason is put in possession of a truth, it does not follow that it may not afford a solid basis on which the reason may construct such a process for itself; and so arrive at even abstract truth, to which without the miracle it could not have attained. We maintain that the miracles of Christ did both demonstrate that the power of God was in him, and furnish the ground for many important deductions in relation to his person. Let us look at the case particularly and see.

We have seen that the miracles of Christ were admitted on all hands to be real. That they were not wrought by merely *human* power was acknowledged also; for this is involved in the very notion of a miracle. But two suppositions then were possible. Either they were wrought as Christ himself affirmed, by the power of God residing in him, or else by the power of the devil, as some of his enemies alleged. The one or the other of these things, it was clear, must be the truth. But the miracles of Christ were all of them, or nearly all, manifestly benevolent in their character, and many of them were in direct and obvious subversion of the dominion and influence of Satan; and the question which Christ asked of those who pretended to ascribe his works to Satanic agency,—"If Satan cast out Satan, how then shall his kingdom stand,"—exposed effectually the absurdity of the idea, that there was any such agency in the case. What then was the inevitable conclusion, to every one who reasoned soundly? Jesus of Nazareth comes as the messenger of God. In proof of his commission he performs these mighty works. They are undeniably beyond all human power. They are palpably opposed to the interests and the spirit of the devil. They do, therefore, evince the truth of what he claims. They do exhibit the power of God as residing in him.

Such, it is clear, was the proper force and bearing of the miracles which were wrought by Jesus Christ. Such was the impression that they were well adapted to produce. It is but a poor sophistry of our modern days that denies their fitness to produce conviction. It was not, therefore, because they were not valid evidence of his Messiahship, that those in whose presence they were wrought did not believe in Jesus. They were the proper credentials of the divinity of his mission.

We come then, in the third place, to observe that the true explanation of the unbelief of those to whom the text relates, must be sought in the state of their own minds as regards their preparation for a right receiving of the evidence, and not in any want of force or adaptation in the evidence itself.

The fact that the effect of evidence depends materially on the internal condition of those to whom it is presented, we may here assume as granted. The clearest light, if the eyes of the understanding be darkened by the influence of perverting causes, may fall almost in vain. Even where the understanding is convinced, the desires and biases of a heart that is corrupt, and the stubbornness of a will that is determined not to yield, may prevent the plainest certainties from being received with a cordial faith. Such are the well-known laws of mental action.

How was it then with those who with all the miracles of Christ before them, refused to believe on him? It is plain, from what we know of the nation generally, and from what the history records of these persons in particular, that they were in a state exceedingly unfavourable to a right appreciation of the personal character of our Lord and to a hearty reception of his spiritual and holy teachings. They were gross and carnal in their views and spirit. Their morality was an outward show, which was worn over the most thorough selfishness. Their religion was rotten at the core—a mere semblance of piety, inspired only by arrogance and pride. They were fully prepossessed with the idea that the Messiah promised to their fathers was to be an entirely different sort of person from what they saw in the Son of Joseph and Mary; and that his advent and career were to be in quite another style than those of Jesus. Looking for one who should restore the Jewish nation, and bring back its ancient glory, they were ill prepared to see in the humble Nazarene the illustrious person whose coming and character had been foretold in the lofty strains of prophets, and longed for by holy patriarchs and kings. Worse than all, when they came to listen to the words of Christ, those words which probed their hearts to the very bottom; when they perceived that his aims were purely spiritual in all his teaching—that to save the lost was the grand object of his mission—that the abandonment of sin, self-sacrifice, and deadness to the world, were the conditions of his discipleship, and that the honours and distinctions which he offered were to be reached only through toil and sufferings, and after the scenes of this earthly life were past; when, I say, they learned all this from the lips of Christ, their hearts were filled, of course, with the most intense repugnance to such a teacher and to such demands.

Here, therefore, there were powerful moral causes to neutralise the force of evidence, and to turn away the mind from the exercise of faith. There was all the strength of prejudices long cherished, and all the antipathy of selfish and unholy hearts, which must be overcome, before they could receive Christ and his doctrines as divine. It was in vain that his purity of character compelled their admiration. It was in vain that the surpassing simplicity and beauty of his doctrines, as well as the more than human authority and power with which he spake, appealed to their consciences and hearts. It was in vain that he clearly showed them, in his expositions of the Scriptures, that the Messianic prophecies all pointed to precisely such a person as himself. It was in vain, that not only in Jerusalem, but throughout the towns and villages of Gallilee, he healed the sick, restored the blind, gave hearing to the deaf, recalled the dead to life, wrought every miracle, in short, for which any occasion offered; and so gave ample demonstration that in him dwelt the power of the Most High. The dislike of the heart prevailed over the force of evidence and perverted the understanding. The obstinacy of the unyielding will resisted the decisions of the conscience. Wicked and highly excited passions disturbed the entire action of the mind, and rendered it morbid and impulsive. In a word, those who rejected Christ, with all his miracles before them, were so completely under the sway of their own corruptions, in bondage to the power of evil, that in this their present moral state there were insurmountable impediments to the right reception of him. The proofs were ample. To pure and upright minds they would have been perfectly convincing. But on them they were lost in a very great degree. They were able, therefore, to struggle successfully against their proper force, and to maintain themselves in spite of them in unbelief. "Therefore they could not believe,"—says the Evangelist in the context,—"because that Esaias said, He hath blinded their eyes, and hardened their heart; that they should not see with their eyes, nor understand with their heart, and be converted, and I should heal them." Left wholly to themselves, no force of evidence could lead them to the right conclusions.

From the examination we have thus given to the particular fact stated in the text, we may derive, as was observed in the beginning, some general truths in which we ourselves have a deep and personal concern.

First of all, we are led to the conclusion that no amount of light shed on the understanding, will, of itself, avail to produce a genuine faith in Christ.

If when the Son of God was on the earth, the very persons who saw him raise up the dead to life by his simple word could still persist in unbelief, then what amount of evidence may not an evil heart resist? If a wrong state of moral feeling could break the force of the proof which the most imposing miracles afforded, what kind or degree of proof can be conceived, which it may not render nugatory?

The truth is, that Christian faith, the faith that rightly relies on Jesus Christ, supposes, along with a convinced understanding, an acquiescing heart and will—the full consent of the voluntary nature. But while the soul is in love with sin, and swayed by selfishness, and averse to the holy, self-denying duties which are included in discipleship, no such consent can ever come from its hidden depths. Let light be poured around it like the blaze of noonday, it will be sure to find some subterfuge wherewith to screen itself. Of this a thousand actual illustrations may easily be found.

Here, then, is seen how great is the delusion of those persons—we fear that there are many of them—who, secretly, or half-unconsciously, perhaps, but really, per suade themselves, that the reason why they do not believe savingly in Christ, is that they need some more *convincing proof* that he is indeed the true and only Saviour. They hear the glorious gospel. They are more or less impressed with the character and works of Jesus Christ. Unlike the Jews, they have no national and traditional prejudices which stand in the way of a general acknowledgment that Christ is the true Messiah, and that Christianity as a system is divine. In short, they have an educational belief, a vague persuasion of the understanding even, resulting from some examination, it may be, of the truth and importance of the peculiar Christian doctrines. But as to the matter of exercising a personal faith in Christ, of personally becoming his hearty and avowed disciples,—they think they cannot do it for want of proofs which should tell with greater power for their conviction. Are there not those in this assembly whose case is now described?—who have imagined that could they but hear a voice immediately from heaven, or could one be sent from the dead to testify to them, as Dives wished, they should then repent and believe the gospel?

Such thoughts are all delusive, certainly. Look at the persons to whom the text refers. Suppose that Dives had actually been sent to them. How could he have furnished stronger evidence that he had come from the world of spirits, than Jesus placed before them, in proof of his divine commission? If unbelief refused to yield in one case, why should it not have refused equally in the other? So in your own case. You have Christ's character, and teachings, and miracles, and all the blessed fruits which Christianity has brought forth in the world for eighteen hundred years before you—and yet you do not believe in Christ to your salvation. What if Gabriel himself were sent to you to-day, with messages all fresh from the throne of God? How could he offer you credentials more decisive than those which Jesus brings? Even if he could, would that remove the difficulties that lie not in the understanding but in the heart? "With the heart," says Paul, "man believeth unto righteousness." Light—testimony—proofs—relate to the understanding. They cannot change the heart. So long as the heart is evil, the understanding will be but partially convinced, most probably; or if it should be wholly, the heart and will would still refuse the consent of cordial faith. So long as your feelings, the moral affections of your souls, continue as they are, you will turn away from Christ, and hold on in unbelief.

This leads us to notice, secondly, the necessity which, from the subject, it is plain exists, that to bring men truly to believe in Christ some rectifying power should be applied directly to the heart. And here there is no uncertainty as to what that power must be. The renewing of the Holy Ghost must be felt within the soul. For this work he has been sent. Under his regenerating power it must be fitted to receive a right impression from the truth; must be set free from the bondage of its pride and prejudice and self-will; must be softened into tenderness, brought into sympathy with what is holy, and so disposed to yield itself with full and ready acquiescence to the evidence which lies before it, that Jesus is the Saviour of the world, and as such worthy of its confidence and love. "No man can come to me," says Christ, "except the Father which hath sent me draw him;" and again, "Except a man be born of the Spirit, he cannot enter into the kingdom of God."

Yes, you, who are waiting for still stronger proofs that Christ is your Redeemer, and that the gospel is divine, here is your great, your absolute necessity. This you, most likely, do not truly feel; but such is undoubtedly the fact. If but the Holy Ghost once breathe on your now stubborn heart, it will thenceforth be soft and yielding. If he take the things of Christ and reveal them unto you, you will no longer be able to resist the overpowering impression of his glory. If he renew a right spirit within you, your tastes and sympathies will no more be obstructions to your faith, but will have become its powerful auxiliaries. Oh, for the coming of that Spirit from above to do this work within you! This is our daily prayer—the prayer of all who have believed—on your behalf. We have no hope from stronger arguments for the truth of our religion; no hope from greater light could it ever be enjoyed. Our hope that you will believe in Christ and live, rests wholly on the promise of the Spirit to convince the world of sin and to regenerate the sinful soul. We will cry, so long as the mercy of God shall spare you, "Come, O breath, from the four winds of heaven, and breathe on these slain, that they may live!"

Of course, we are able to see plainly, in the last place, how utterly hopeless, though living in the midst of the most precious Christian privileges, are those from whom the Holy Spirit is withdrawn.

That he was at length withdrawn from the unbelieving Jews is certain. Jesus himself wept over them in view of the distressing fact: "Oh, if thou hadst known, even thou, in this thy day, the things that belong to thy peace; but now they are *hidden* from thine eyes!" That he is now withdrawn from many who still enjoy the gospel, there is painful reason to believe. The Scriptures clearly intimate this as true; and "Grieve not the Spirit," "Quench not the Spirit," are the warning voices which they raise; while the moral deadness in which so many live and die are affecting comments on their teachings. Of course, as light alone, however clear, will never bring them to believe in Christ; as the Holy Ghost alone is able to accomplish this, the moment he finally departs from them, the last hope of their eternity goes out in utter darkness.

Perhaps while we were just now saying, that there was an absolute necessity that the Holy Spirit of God should rightly dispose the heart—your heart—in order to the exercise of genuine faith, the question was suggested to your thoughts, Why then does he not come, and perform the necessary work in me? You even think, perhaps, that you desire he would, and are waiting that he may. Why, then, in reality does he not? Without attempting to pry into things which are not revealed, perhaps we can learn something on this point. Why does he not do his peculiar work in you?

Did you ever earnestly entreat him that he would? Did you ever go to him in your solitary place to tell him of all the blindness, the carnality, the perverseness of your heart, and beg him with self-abasement and with tears to change it? Have you ever seriously sought to withdraw your heart from worldliness and folly, and to yield it to the Spirit that he might mould it at his will? Or if you have ever done these things, have you done them with a deep concern and a determined perseverance?

If not, what need have you to raise the question, Why the Holy Spirit does not come to do his renovating work in you? Why should he? If you are not sufficiently concerned to seek his saving help; if you will neither invite him to your heart, nor open it to give him entrance; are not these good reasons for his absence, whatever others there may be? It is not surely to be wondered at, in such a case, that he does not renew your soul. Nor will it be, if being long neglected and resisted he withdraws from you for ever, and leaves you in the hopeless state of those who with all the mighty miracles of Christ before them, persisted still in their unbelief.

Ah—it is true, you who, with the clearest light, do not believe in Christ, that you tread on perilous ground. It is a renovated, holy heart you want—a heart touched by the Holy Ghost. The provisions of the gospel are not without conditions. It is *to them that ask Him*, that your heavenly Father is more willing to give the Holy Spirit, than parents are to give good things unto their children. But you ask not, seek not, knock not, at the door of mercy. Oh, take ye heed, lest ye be left to the fatal quiet which follows the final withdrawment of the divine Spirit from the soul. Come while he urges you to believe in Christ and live!

XII.

The Dark Things of Life in the Light of Revelation.

1 KINGS xvi. 22: *So Tibni died, and Omri reigned.*

IT is a strange world in which we live. About us, on all sides, a thousand things are constantly occurring, which but for the fact that we have been familiar with such events from childhood, would startle and astonish us; and which do, even as it is, sometimes occasion many troubled thoughts in sober and reflecting minds.

Our circle of observation, too, is very limited. We see but little of the whole field of human life and action as our own time presents it; to say nothing of the great history of humanity considered as extending through all ages. But if, by some supernatural aid, we could be gifted with the power to see at once all that is actually transpiring in the fortunes of mankind; or if some swift-winged angel be imagined as making a full survey of all, there would, of course, be seen to be vastly more to excite one's wonder, in this all-embracing view, than falls at present within our observation. No words could give an adequate impression of the scenes which would be witnessed. Omri, ascending the throne, may be regarded as representing the extreme of fortune, on the favourable side, since men are wont to count a throne the pinnacle of earthly prosperity and glory. Tibni, on the other hand, may be taken as representing the opposite, or unfavourable extreme; since death is reckoned, by common consent, the greatest of all the ills which a human being is liable to suffer. Between these two extremes—that of rising to the highest summit of worldly splendour and delight, and that of sinking to the dreariness of death and of the grave—an infinite number and variety of incidents are momentarily occurring to the millions of mankind. If all the passing expressions of human thought and feeling to which these incidents are giving rise, could be conveyed together to one ear, who can conceive the confusion and discords of the mighty chorus so produced? Words of tenderness and love, mingling with those of malignity and hate; exclamations of ecstatic pleasure, blending with groans of anguish and despair; voices of wisdom, delivering itself in high discourse, and of folly, sensuality, and sin, giving utterances of shame and guilt; sounds of revelry and dancing, of pipe, and tabret, and song, of brilliant talk and of pealing laughter, along with the shrieks of the insane, the wail of thousands stretched on the gory battle-fields of nations, the low murmurs of death-beds, and the sobs of broken-hearted weepers, gathered round them;—all these and more, in one commingled volume, would strike the stunned and bewildered sense. They all *are* actually heard together every moment by the ear of the omnipresent God.

Or if it can be conceived that all the countless phases of human fortune which belong to any given day or hour, should be at once presented to the eye of one observer, no pen of man or angel can portray the mingled lights and shades of the astounding picture. Whoever chooses may try his own imagination in the effort to realize it to himself. But we will not attempt even to sketch a faint and general outline, of what is really beyond all human power, not merely of description, but even of thought itself.

It is certainly no wonder, then, that life is so often pronounced a mystery. To the view of natural reason unassisted, it is a mystery, dark, perplexing, and insoluble. Yes; without the light which revelation throws upon it, the more one knows of life, the wider his experience of its vicissitudes, the more profoundly mysterious it is. We ask in vain of reason, Whence all these painful contrasts, this confusion, this singular medley of good and evil? But with the Bible in our hands, we do obtain at least a partial satisfaction. If we cannot fully solve the problem of human life as the world actually presents it everywhere, we may assure ourselves beyond all doubt that we have found the clue to the true solution. We may find some lifting of the shadows which rest on the condition of humanity; we may discover, even in life's strangest spectacles, some lessons of instruction well worthy of our serious attention. This, then, is what we now propose: to lead the way in some reflections on *the mutability of human fortunes*, as contemplated in the light of our divine religion; in doing which, of course, we assume as granted, the being, perfection, and universal government of God, and the reality of a positive revelation.

The first fact which presents itself, when we consider the singular diversities of human fortune from the position now defined, is this—that human life, as it actually appears, is plainly not in harmony with the government and will of God. Mankind are not, in other words, what God, in their creation, fitted them to be, and what in his providence he has given them ample opportunity to become. Gifted with freedom; adapted to virtuous action and enjoyment; surrounded with means of physical, intellectual, and moral culture, instructed as to their relations to God, and their obligations to obey him; the race, by the abuse of their high endowments, opportunities, and knowledge, have come into bondage to appetite and sense, and placed themselves in a state of alienation from God, and antagonism to his authority and law. With the views of the divine character and government which the Bible furnishes before us, the moral apostasy and ruin of mankind, the debasement and degeneracy of their condition, the two great facts, in a word, that they are a sinful race, and that as such they deserve to suffer evil, are clear and undeniable. Man has himself a responsibility in relation to his own welfare—a power, within certain limits, to determine his own fortunes; and the Scriptures say of the race that they have all gone out of the way, have together become unprofitable, so that there is none that doeth good, no, not one. Some more, and some less entirely, they have yielded themselves to evil; but all, as alike estranged from God, are justly liable to bear the penalties of sin.

Now, when we look with pain at the vanity of human life—at the instability of its joys, the multiplicity of its sorrows, and the affecting vicissitudes which it presents—we are never to forget that this condition of things is, to a very great extent, the result of the folly and madness of mortal men themselves. If we examine the structure of our own being, or the constitution and course of nature, we shall not find in either anything to make it necessary that life should be the empty affair it too generally is. "Thou hast made him but little lower than the angels," said the psalmist, when he considered the noble faculties of man. So when he surveyed the order, and beauty, and benevolent adjustments of the natural world, he broke out in the language of profound admiration: "O Lord, how manifold are thy works! In wisdom has thou made them all. The earth is full of thy riches." Man is constitutionally capable of a far higher and better life than that which now he leads; within his reach are richer and more enduring enjoyments than those which now he ordinarily attains. Did he but live in harmony with the will of the Creator, there would still indeed be varieties of fortune, but only varieties of good and happy fortune; and not the painful contrasts, the mixture of good and evil, which we at present everywhere observe.

Here, then, in this fundamental fact of human sinfulness, we have certainly some light on the dark problem which the chequered and ever shifting aspect of mortal life presents. The oppressive feeling which naturally arises when we regard our race as doomed to live amidst perpetual contingencies and change—a feeling that prompts the query in our minds whether or not they are justly dealt with—is most materially relieved when we are brought to estimate their characters and merits by the test of a perfect moral law. If we were conscious that we ourselves were innocent, and believed that the same was true of mankind at large, our moral sense would doubtless pronounce our earthly lot unrighteously severe. Our sense of justice would rise up against the providential government of God. But once let us admit that we are guilty in the sight of God—unworthy of unmingled favour at his hand—and conscience takes at once the other side. It tells us that our measure of good is, after all, *far greater than we deserve.* There is no more room for complaining thoughts. We cannot help perceiving that the painful mutability of human happiness on earth is quite consistent with the infinite benevolence of God. We may observe one rising and another falling every hour; we may pass ourselves through all varieties of fortune, and yet find no good ground on which to impeach the wisdom or the justice of the Supreme Ruler of the world. A *sinful* world may well be a world of inconstant fortunes, of interrupted and precarious happiness.

A second fact which throws light on the problem presented by the inconstancy of human fortunes, is that the present life is but the prelude or initiatory stage of an existence without end.

With the Scriptures in our hands the doctrine of immortality is settled. That the chief scene of our existence lies beyond that strange event which we call death, is now as certain as any fact of natural science. Yet it is far more difficult to give it practical reality to our minds. We are in bondage to mere sense; and it is hard for us to rid ourselves of its illusions. It is difficult to rise above the habit into which we naturally incline to fall, of judging of this life as though it were to be considered by itself; as though death were a real, and not simply an apparent termination of our being—a transition only from one stage to another.

Now, it will easily be seen that it must make a mighty difference, in our views of the events of the present life, whether we regard it *as a whole in itself*, or only as a *preliminary part*, standing related to a far more grand and interesting sequel afterwards to come. No wonder that the lot of mortals appears mysterious and gloomy, considered as a complete existence. A few years swiftly fleeting by; childhood, youth, manhood, age, succeeding each other like the changes of a dream; and all exhibiting every imaginable diversity of fortune—here smiles and there tears; now successes and now reverses; this moment hope, the next despair; a throne to-day, a grave to-morrow. What is there in such an existence to satisfy? What is there worth the having? Listen to the language of one who, denying revelation, could take no other view of life but this. "In man," says Voltaire, "there is more wretchedness than in all the other animals put together. He loves life, yet he knows that he must die. If he enjoys a transient good, he suffers various evils, and is at last devoured by worms. This knowledge—of his end—is his fatal prerogative; other animals have it not. He spends the transient moments of existence in diffusing the miseries which he suffers; in cutting the throats of his fellow-creatures for pay; in cheating and being cheated; in robbing and being robbed; in serving that he might command; and in repenting of all he does. The bulk of mankind are nothing more than a crowd of wretches, equally criminal and unfortunate; and the globe contains rather carcasses than men. I tremble at this dreadful picture to find that it contains a complaint against Providence itself; and I wish I had never been born!" Ah, wretched man! Such are the miseries of unbelief. Such are the views of life which are likely to be taken by those who see in it no relation to an immortal life beyond.

But this dismal picture changes its aspect at once, when by the aid of revelation we put the present in its true relation to the future. With this illumination falling around us from above, the events of these mortal years acquire a new significance. Now, we perceive that this our brief career on earth, is not our *life*—but only a *few moments*, as it were, introductory to that life.

"O listen man!
A voice within us speaks the startling words,
Man—thou shalt *never* die! Celestial voices
Hymn it around our souls: according harps,
By angel fingers touched, when the mild stars
Of morning sang together, sound forth still
The song of our great immortality.
O listen, ye our spirits; drink it in
From all the air! 'tis in the gentle moonlight;
'Tis floating in day's setting glories; Night
Wrapped in her sable robe, with silent step
Comes to our bed and breathes it in our ears."

Thus assured, and constantly reminded of the vastness of our being, it seems less singular, most certainly, that this first stage of it should necessarily involve some temporary discomforts and privations, to say nothing here of the mischiefs wrought by sin. It may obviously be true that there are good reasons why, for this transient preparatory period, enjoyment—happiness—should not be the chief thing to be secured. When a young man is placed by his parents in the condition of an apprentice, the main object is not to make him *happy* during the limited term of years for which he serves. On the contrary, it is distinctly understood that, for the sake of the *future years of life,* he is, for the present, to submit to many sacrifices; to bear patiently not a few self-denials and privations; and even possibly some actual hardships. Why, then, should it be wondered at, if in this brief apprenticeship of ours on earth, this first short scene of an interminable existence, it should not seem to be the design of Providence to make us *completely happy;* if, on the contrary, it should subject us to many trials and discomforts. Why should it not be rationally believed, that so many, at least, of the adversities which mark our lives as are fairly to be attributed to the providence of God, are fitted to subserve some ends, in reference to the future, far more important than that of giving us a present pleasure? And if this be admitted, then from this point of view, there are some cheering rays to gild the troubled waters of life's ever-restless sea. The terrible picture drawn by the pen of unbelief, which we have quoted, is seen to be essentially a false one; and the fortunes of humanity, inconstant and in many aspects painful as they are, seem far less mysterious and gloomy than before.

We come then to a third fact, namely, that considering life as a school of discipline with reference to character, its perpetual vicissitudes materially help to adapt it to its end.

We have just had occasion to observe, that during a short initiatory period of our being, it may well be that happiness should be regarded, as, for the time, only a secondary thing; and we have now further to add, what in the light of the word of God we are very sure is true, that the whole economy of things pertaining to our condition in this world, is arranged primarily with a view to the formation of right character. In this the divine wisdom and goodness are alike apparent. For in right character, and in this alone, can the foundations of solid and enduring happiness be laid.

In order to right character, there must be discipline. It is difficult for us to conceive that even a race of beings commencing their existence in a state of innocence, should develop virtuous and holy character, in maturity and strength without the discipline of trials. Certainly to a sinful race like ours, it is plain that even a severe regimen for a season may be, if not absolutely indispensable, at least eminently fitted to prove useful, as a means of such development.

Painful, therefore, as it may be to contemplate the vanity of mortal life as seen in the instability of human fortunes, and the diversities of human condition, it cannot be denied that this very state of things exhibits a wise and good arrangement, for the attainment of a most important end.

How is it, for example, that mankind are most effectually awakened from the dreams of a mere sensual and selfish life, and brought to some serious reflection on themselves and on their duties? Is it not by the discovery that the visions of pleasure which have looked to them so enchanting and so real, are all vanishing around them, as the golden hues of sunset fade while yet they are admired? How is it that men become most thoroughly convinced that the riches, the renown, the distinctions, the power, and all the manifold forms of worldly good, are by no means the highest and best objects of desire? Is it not by the experience, or the observation, of the disappointments which attend the pursuit, and the dissatisfaction and uncertainty connected with the full possession of them? What seems so likely to lead men to feel their dependence upon God, and to resort to him as willing to become their Father, Friend, and portion, as the want of sympathy they feel—and the need of something stable to confide in—when all around them is like the shifting sands, and nothing gives them rest? What nurses all the kindly virtues like contact with the suffering, or being ourselves the sufferers? How, but in the struggles which life-long must be waged with capricious fortune, to wrest from her the successes to be gained, or to surmount the adversities to be endured, are all the manly energies of virtuous character and holy principle to be called forth into strength?

Yes, if we seriously consider, we shall see that by the instability of human fortunes which, on the first impression, seems to cover life with gloom, there is supplied a necessary and most salutary discipline. By this it is that life is fitted to become to every one a noble school in which to shape the character, and to secure the highest and best training of the soul. Ease, quiet, uninterrupted pleasures, would be nearly or quite certain, if constantly enjoyed through a course of years, to beget weakness of purpose, the love of self-indulgence, and a sensual and slothful spirit. It is in the stern conflicts of life which grow out of its mutations; in the wrestlings with adversity, which rouse all the faculties to action, and gird up the whole man to the utmost energy of effort; that patience, courage, confidence in God, and constancy to the sense of duty, with other kindred virtues, are best originated and matured.

It remains, in the fourth place, to notice one fact more. It is that over all the fluctuations and diversities of human fortune, God exercises an unceasing and intelligent superintendence, directed to the end of working out the good of those who intrust their happiness to him. Of this deeply interesting fact the word of revelation makes us sure.

When we look at the spectacle of life—at its vast gradation of conditions, and its never ceasing changes—we are half inclined to feel that it is a world of chance in which we live. It almost seems as if we ourselves, and others, were left the sport of accident, like bubbles on a stormy sea, driven hither and thither by the ever-varying tempest. To think this were a great mistake. Under such conditions it were indeed a wretched thing to live.

Instead of this, we know that in all the countless mutations of human things, there is not one, which God does not himself directly order, or for wise purposes permit. We know that God, having, by the provision of abundant mercy through Jesus Christ, his Son, invited men to come in their conscious guilt and weakness, and put their trust in him, has also pledged himself to make all things work together for good to them that do so. We know that Jesus, the Redeemer and sufficient Saviour of the world, has bound himself, as the faithful shepherd, to go before his own, and to keep them unto life eternal. We hear him promise that in the midst of outward tribulations, in him they should have peace; and that he will not leave them comfortless, but will come unto them.

This, then, we know with certainty; that whatever may be, to human view, the fickleness of fortune; however many and great the vicissitudes which every day may bring; those who shall come at the call of mercy and make the eternal God their refuge, shall never suffer one reverse to their real detriment; shall never see one hope lie shattered to their harm; shall never have one tear too many for their good wrung from them; shall never feel one pang that shall not minister to their intenser joy at last. God, who is able to bring good out of evil, will so direct all changes of their lot, that even from the tossings of the fitful sea of life, there shall eventually come to them more perfect and serene repose.

Here, indeed, a flood of light breaks in upon the shaded scene of life. In all the shifting acts of the ever changing drama, the agency of God is present directing all things to the end of blessing those who are willing to be blest. There is no real blindness of fortune, as men have fabled, after all. There *is* no fortune but the providence of God. It is God that setteth up. It is God that casteth down. It is he that hath pronounced those blessed always and everywhere, who heartily commit the care of their happiness to him.

We are not, then, you perceive, condemned to brood in hopeless melancholy over the vanity and transitoriness of the pursuits and hopes of this mortal life. We are not like the hapless denier of revealed religion, to see in the condition of mankind only unmitigated evil, and in view of it to cast reproach on the great Ruler of the world. If the human race is sinful, they involve themselves in suffering and deserve it. If life is a short preparatory season with reference to an endless being, it may naturally involve the necessity of present crosses; if it is meant to be a school of discipline, it is clearly well adapted to its purpose. If God presides over all the vicissitudes of fortune, to work out good for all who confide in him, those who accept his guardianship have nothing at all to fear. In all events, from the mounting to a throne to the putting on of grave clothes, their interests shall alike be safe. When, therefore, we observe or reflect upon the changes that in the lot of man so rapidly succeed each other, and at all the diversities of condition that everywhere appear, we are to feel that we have at least a partial illumination of the mystery of life; we are to look on it with unfaltering confidence in the benevolence of God; and especially we are to study anxiously the responsibilities which it imposes upon us, in cheerful hope and faithful effort, to rise to a state of stable and perfected happiness at a future period of our being.

Let us, then, fix it in our minds, for this is the great practical lesson of our subject, that *not* to understand the true nature and design of life, as shown us in the Scriptures, is the greatest of calamities. Since the chief value of the present state of being depends on its being a place in which the punishment of sin is for a while delayed—a place of preparation and discipline for the eternal future—a place in which the love and care of God is pledged to work out good to them that love him,—if we thoughtlessly neglect to notice this and act accordingly, we endure the trials and miss all the useful ends of living here. Ah! how many do this in their folly! It *is* the height of folly to mistake this fleeting, shadowy, unsatisfying scene of things for the scene of our *full existence!* When we regard it in this light—when we try to rear the structure of our welfare on these false, sliding quicksands—we doom ourselves to disappointments without solace, to painful labours without any adequate reward. Oh, rather let us thankfully accept the light that infinite love has made to stream from heaven on our path. "I am the light of the world," saith the blessed Son of God. Yes, *he* hath brought life and immortality to light! HE hath given us exceeding great and precious promises. HE is the Rock of Ages, on which, where all else is unstable, we may build our hopes securely. HE hath engaged to wipe all the tears of those who accept and follow him, far—far away from these transitory scenes, where he will make them speedily forget the sufferings here endured, in the solid, changeless, pure delights of heaven! In Christ alone, and in his gospel, is the *true solution* for us of *life's great mystery.* If we fail to avail ourselves of this, we may reign, we may die, we may pass through all the vicissitudes that lie between—but "vanity of vanities" will be the record of our experience; and we shall end our sad career in a darkness to which there shall never, never be a dawn! From this may Eternal Love preserve us!

XIII.

The Gospel the Sole Hope of the World.

MARK xvi. 15: *"And he saith unto them, Go ye into all the world and preach the gospel to every creature."*

ACCEPTING the Christian revelation, we accept, of course, the grand fact which it announces—that Christ came to save the world. It needed saving then. The whole significance and value of his mission must stand on the previous fact that mankind were in a state of moral ruin—a state as to any power of self-recovery absolutely hopeless. Not by any means that the race had lost the God-like constitutional endowments which they originally received—the intellect, the conscience, the yearning of a spiritual nature, and that freedom of will which lays the foundation for a just accountability. Not that every semblance of good, every kind, and amiable, and praiseworthy trait of character had disappeared. The truth, precisely stated, was that the race had fallen from a state of innocence under law, were individually condemned to die, and were so subjected to the power of evil propensity and appetite, that the tendency to a deeper and deeper degradation was universal and decisive. To deny that such was the actual condition of mankind is to deny that such a mission as that of the divine Founder of Christianity was necessary; yet more, it is in effect to affirm that it was an uncalled for and mistaken pity that moved the eternal Father when he so loved the world as to give his only begotten Son, that whosoever believeth on him might not perish.

As with right views of the character of Jesus Christ it is not to be doubted that he rightly understood the necessities of those for whose sake he became incarnate, so neither can we doubt that in his work for their deliverance he did precisely what the case demanded. We conclude also, with certainty, that when, on leaving the world, he gave it in charge to his disciples to prosecute to its full accomplishment the work of the world's recovery to spiritual life and soundness, the means which he directed them to use were, in like manner, those which would be found most effectual to the end.

What, then, did the divine Redeemer prescribe as the effectual remedy for the sad condition of mankind? He simply commanded his apostles to preach the gospel, connecting with this, as we learn by a comparison of texts, the two Christian sacraments, by the observance of which his followers might be recognised and his Church have an organic and visible existence. A wonderful success attended their faithful obedience to his word. That the world is no purer and no happier at this distance of time is to be ascribed to the fact that their successors in the Christian ministry have not steadily and faithfully followed in their steps. The full experiment of the prescription has, therefore, never yet been made. It is to be made, however. The Christian Church is charged to make it, and now deliberately accepts the work; and I design, in the present discourse, to insist on the thought which the text, taken in its relations, fairly sets before us —that the administration of the gospel and its ordinances is the sole hope of the world.

You will at once perceive that the first step towards a just illustration of this topic must be to state explicitly what, in our apprehension of the matter, the essential gospel is. We say the *essential* gospel, for we suppose that the Christian Scriptures set forth many truths of great interest in themselves, which yet are not so essentially a part of Christianity as a ministration of life, that without them it loses its vital power. That is the essential gospel, on which, directly and specially, the saving energy of Christianity depends. It is the more necessary to speak on this point with distinctness, because that in the entire freedom of opinion and of speech which is one of our national birth-rights, it has sometimes happened of late that the deism of Bolingbroke and Hume, and even a close approximation to downright atheism, have been promulgated from the pulpit and misnamed Christianity. But hemlock is still hemlock, though you should choose to call it balm; and if we receive under the name of God's appointed means of life that which in fact is noxious, we are sure to find at length that words cannot change the reality of things.

We say, then, distinctly that the gospel which has been divinely prescribed as the remedy for the guilt and misery of our race is the offer of forgiveness, spiritual renovation, and permanent favour with God, on the basis of a redemption effected by the incarnation, sufferings, and death of the Lord Jesus Christ, and through the mission and agency of the Holy Ghost, the Comforter. God can and will forgive the penitent. God can and will renew and sanctify. God can and will adopt into his family and confer all the privileges of sonship. These are the primary truths of the essential gospel—these the glad tidings addressed to the human race as defiled, enslaved, and disinherited by sin. Tell these things to the dying, and you let in the light of hope on their dark and despairing souls. Give these elementary truths, and from them the whole system of doctrine and duty which the New Testament expounds may be developed in its completeness and proportion. Withhold these and you withhold the real gospel, profess to teach it as you may. Though your speech be as the melody of waters—though it sparkle with the pregnancy of wit, the elegance of learning, and the quaintness of conceit—though it arrogate to itself preeminent independence, originality, and power of argument, and profess, ever so confidently, the ability to exalt mankind,—it will, after all, have neither the essence nor the energy of genuine Christianity. It may divert men for a time, but cannot in the least avail to heal their inward maladies; and their hearts unreached, uncured, will secretly bleed on.

You will notice, also, that the power of the gospel, according to the view of its radical truths just given, is an internal and spiritual power. It is not a ministry of forms addressed to the outward sense; but of purifying and restoring influences—of vital energy applied to the disordered and morally debased and enfeebled soul. In this respect, it differs widely from Judaism, and from the false systems which human wisdom, or folly, has contrived, and is immeasurably higher and nobler than either the former or the latter. To attempt to connect with the admirable simplicity of Christian truth, imposing outward pomps and ceremonies, is to forget the very genius of Christianity. It is just to descend from the sublime elevation on which our Lord has placed us by that memorable declaration, " God is a spirit, and they that worship him must worship him in spirit and in truth," to the sensuous and every way inferior externalism of the legal dispensation. Judaism prescribed its gorgeous robes, its rich adornings, and its grand processions and pageantries in the worship of Jehovah. Christianity says simply, "Let all things be done decently and in order. Judaism exacted costly offerings; Christianity demands a contrite heart. Judaism pointed the conscience-stricken sinner to a material temple, a smoking altar, and a sprinkling priest; Christianity bids him "behold the Lamb of God!" Judaism made great account of a natural descent from Abraham; Christianity insists on being born of the Spirit of God. Judaism was exclusive, regarding those within its own circle as especially admitted to God's favour; Christianity, in the largeness of its charity, declares that God is no respecter of persons, but that, everywhere, he that feareth him and worketh righteousness is accepted of him. Judaism accepted, as evidence of superior piety, a lively zeal for outward observances, such as washings, fasts, and feasts; Christianity instructs that genuine piety consists in no such things as these, but in righteousness and peace, and joy in the Holy Ghost.

Such is the gospel as a saving power. It is a leaven that works from within outwardly. Its words are spirit and life. It is strong in its divine simplicity. It has no affinity for imposing rites and ceremonies, and is only obstructed and degraded by them. When, therefore, we affirm that the gospel and its ordinances are the world's sole hope, we mean to affirm that it is the preaching of these simple and divinely energetic truths to which we have alluded, accompanied with the two Christian sacraments, and disencumbered of all unnecessary outward form, that is God's appointed instrumentality, for the raising up of debased humanity to life and virtue, to holiness and solid peace.

With this brief statement of what the gospel is conceived to be in its elemental truths, we proceed directly to the confirmation of the general statement that in it lies the only hope of a sinning and suffering world.

We here take, as the ground of the whole argument, the nature of the evils to be cured. It is true, we apprehend, that but few persons, comparatively, even among the most thoughtful and enlightened, are accustomed to contemplate these evils in their full extent and import. We see and admit that the condition of mankind is in many respects a sad one; but from our infancy we have been familiar with all its painful aspects. We have never known by experience a happier state than that which we see to be the lot of our mortal race at present, and are not able, therefore, to judge of what we are, by comparison with what we were, or with what we might now have been. But suppose we make a thorough examination of the case.

Suppose we start the question, with a view to find for ourselves an answer, how men compare in character and happiness with angels, and earth as an abode with heaven. At once an appalling disparity appears. In the one case, everything is perfect, in the other absolutely nothing. But why this mighty difference? Whence is it that this world, so glorious in its structure and adornings, so radiant with the beauty of the Infinite, is not the abode of perfect life and joy? As respects their intellectual and moral nature, men claim affinity with angels; why are they not complete in their development and blest in their estate, like them? These questions would lead us to the whole melancholy truth. We are apt to rest satisfied with the general and very vague admission that sin has disturbed the harmony which should subsist between God and man, and that it may be necessary, by way of preparation for a future life, that something should be done to adjust the difference. It *is*, indeed, the prime difficulty in the case, that the individual soul is broken off from God by the transgression of his law. It *is* a momentous fact that every human being has need to prepare for the retributions of the eternal state. But these statements are only a fragment of the truth. If we would state the whole, we must say that the blighting effects of sin extend to man's entire nature, to all his social and moral relations, and all the circumstances of his being. Nothing in himself, nothing in his fellowship with others, nothing in the state of things around him, is what it would have been, had he not become a sinner. Either really, or in relation to his feelings, everything is changed.

Look, for instance, at the body, that wonderful piece of mechanism. Whence its liability to so many derangements, its infirmities, its pains, its decay, and final dissolution? Because of sin it is condemned to return to dust; and, more or less remotely, it receives the recompense of irregular appetite and lawless passion in disease and suffering; so that while, for aught that appears, it might have been always elastic, fresh, and youthful, a fit organ for the spirit, it has come to be a shattered and perishable thing. Look at the intellectual nature also. It seems almost angelic in its constitutional powers; and yet how far it is, in fact, from a perfect condition and a healthful and vigorous activity! It is, in by far the greater number of cases, but very imperfectly unfolded and disciplined, and in not a few instances is developed scarcely at all. It is beclouded with the fogs of prejudice, encumbered by biases, cheated by the vagaries of its own fancy, duped by superstition, and rendered grovelling by sensual inclinations. Look, further still, at the moral sensibilities, made to appreciate the morally right, and true, and beautiful, with an immediate and just perception, and to be delicately susceptible to the impression of moral obligation. In the great mass of men they are either perverted altogether, or rendered so blunt and torpid that they exhibit their proper results but in a very slight degree. Observe, finally, the social affections. They were given to bind each by tender affinities to all his kind. They were intended to originate and maintain sweet charities among such as are joined by the ties of kindred, and to spread over all the pathways of life an atmosphere of benevolence and love. But what vast portions of mankind in all past ages, and in our own as well, have known nothing, or next to nothing, of the pleasures of pure friendship, nothing of domestic joys; but have lived in social discord and corruption, possessed with evil passions, and being destroyers of each other's peace. Remember we are speaking of mankind in their natural condition; as Christianity has found them, not as it has made them when it has been cordially received. No one, certainly, who is acquainted with the history, or the present condition of mankind, can hesitate to admit that man is spiritually estranged from God; and that, in body, in intellect, in his moral sensibilities, in his natural affections, in short, throughout his entire being and his whole condition in the world, he suffers the effects of sin, and is subject to its power.

Yes, go where paganism has had its seat, where the dogmas of false prophets and religionists have wrought out their results, where sensuous pomps and human traditions have corrupted and obscured the truth, and where infidelity, with its boast of superior wisdom, has cast out faith of every kind; and there will be found in all these circumstances a moral degradation of humanity which reaches into every sphere of its activity, and penetrates every ramification of its interests. It is only a literal truth—except so far as the influence of Christianity has been practically felt—that the whole creation groaneth and travaileth in pain together until now. The splendid civilizations of antiquity were only gilded aggregations of individual and social profligacy, and literally rotted in their own corruptions. The immensely populous nations of modern Asia are sunk in a debasement so complete that but few traces of anything really noble in our nature are exhibited among them. Africa, taken altogether, is if possible in yet a worse condition. Even in the most favoured portions of Europe and America, how vast the amount of such evils as result from moral degeneracy are yet to be removed before any near approximation to a state of general well-being can be reached! We refer here only to facts which, to all well-informed persons, are perfectly familiar.

The bearing of these acknowledged facts, it will be seen, is this. The mischiefs which sin has wrought, both in separating the individual soul from God, and in deranging the whole economy of human society and human life, are plainly so great, so general, so deep-seated, and inveterate, that there is not the smallest reason to think that the race ever would, or ever could, indeed, restore and purify itself. In the nature of the case, there is a plain necessity that some remedy should be applied of far mightier efficacy than belongs to any of those that lie within the range of man's own feeble powers. He could never, for himself, make peace with God, nor break from his own neck the miserable yoke of sin, nor regulate the conflicting moral elements within him, nor wake in his soul those pure desires which alone could bear him on to a real exaltation.

In accordance with this reasoning from the nature of human wants, is the important fact which we now notice, in the next place, that every attempt permanently to elevate and bless mankind by merely human instrumentalities and efforts has resulted in disastrous failure. Experiment on experiment has been made. Never finding rest, but always like the troubled sea, humanity has reached in this direction and in that, and has had recourse to a variety of means in order to elevate itself. When individual man, oppressed with a sense of his own sad state, scourged by conscience, weary with the chase of shadows, pining with the hunger of an empty craving heart, has sought for some effectual relief, philosophy has discoursed to him sagaciously of the *summum bonum!* She has led him, wondering and bewildered, through all her subtle mazes; has perhaps amused him with beautiful theories of morals; but she has left him, in the end, as unsatisfied and wretched as before, because, failing, utterly, to give him what he wanted. False systems of religion have put him at the task of gaining inward peace by the voluntary subjection of himself to outward suffering. On this track he has fled from the face of his fellow-men. In the depths of the lonely wilderness, or in the murky caves of unfrequented mountains, he has fixed his cheerless dwelling. He has spread his pallet with thorns and lacerated his flesh with knotted scourges; has watched, fasted, and mortified even his innocent desires; and stifling the pleadings of nature in his heart, has sacrificed his own children to avert apprehended wrath and purchase inward peace. But has he gained his object by such means? He may have quieted in some degree the accusings of a bewildered and perverted conscience; but has he made himself a happy, a complete, and morally exalted being? Never. Every such expedient has proved vain.

Nor has legislation ever been found effectual for the

relief and the moral culture of mankind. It has, indeed, accomplished many useful things. It has studied with attention, and often no doubt profoundly, the problems that concern the well-being of society. It has digested codes of laws and arranged the details of administration, with great sagacity and labour; and has tried now this experiment of political economy, and now that. It has striven to balance the conflicting powers and to harmonize the discordant passions and interests of the various classes that compose the state. It has prescribed to men their style of dress, their recreations, their secular pursuits, their divinities and modes of worship. But, after all, the good effects of legislation have been extremely limited in comparison with the evils to be remedied; and revolutions, anarchies, and popular debasement, have too often interrupted its action and defeated its designs. So in regard to other similar agencies. Poetry and eloquence have essayed to refine individual man and to elevate the aims and the spirit of society. They have sought to accomplish this by presenting to the thought ideal beauty and perfection; by thrilling the sensibilities with the flow of harmonious numbers; by stirring the deep emotions of the soul to high enthusiasm, and urging it to lofty undertakings by the force of sweet persuasion. Something has doubtless been achieved by these and kindred agencies, at certain times and to a moderate extent; yet they have been, at best, but as stars above a stormy ocean, that shed some gleams of light upon the surface, but have not power to penetrate its depths, and still less to lull its agitations to repose.

In what is here asserted we are sustained by the voice of universal history. Its explicit testimony is, that while the causes to which we have referred, and others like them, have had an important influence on human things, they have never been able, either separately or combined, to raise and purify, and generally and effectually to bless mankind. This is the melancholy record for all nations and for every age. The thousand sages and moralists of ancient and modern times may have conceived and spoken well on many points of doctrine and of duty. But what then? They spoke, it is certain, without authority to give weight to their instructions; without simplicity to render them intelligible; without the certainty that what they taught was true; and without that adaptation to the hearts and consciences, to the nature and the wants of men, which alone could give them access to the unreflecting multitude. The Jeromes, the Antonies, and the Basils of corrupt Christianity, the ascetics of Persia, and the further East, may be allowed to have uttered just and useful precepts on deadness to the world and religious retirement and meditation. But the attempt to impart true spiritual life and peace to the souls of men by such methods as they exemplified and recommended, was always found to be as futile in experiment as it was absurd in its idea. The Solons and Numas, the Justinians and Alfreds, of all ages, have certainly exhibited great practical wisdom, and often, perhaps, have done all that the nature of the case admitted, in giving laws and framing constitutions. But the fact is undeniable, that human passion has proved to be beyond the control of laws. By no fault of theirs as statesmen and legislators, it has laughed to scorn their nicely adjusted systems, and the floods of licentiousness have gone over their checks and barriers, and have swept them all away. The masses of mankind have neither been lifted from their debasement nor made happy by their labours. With the fact before us that the great masters of eloquence and poetry have breathed forth glorious utterances, words of beauty and of power that have embodied noble thoughts and have sounded through the ages, the other fact, that they have been appreciated, and even recognised only by the comparatively few, is also too plain to be denied. This unequivocal testimony of all history, that the illustrious individual men of different ages, who, from their personal endowments, or the eminence of their position, have seemed most likely to succeed in the attempt to elevate and purify mankind, have never in reality succeeded; and that the advancement of the race has been mainly in connection with Christianity, at once demonstrates the insufficiency of merely human means, and makes it plain that if there is any hope at all that the world will ever be brought to a state of general virtue, intelligence, and happiness, Christianity in its essential truths, in other words, the simple gospel of Jesus Christ, must furnish the ground on which it rests.

We reach, then, at this point, the third part of the argument; wherein we have to show that the gospel, as prescribed by the Son of God, does in fact embody in it all the elements of moral power that are required in order to the raising of the whole family of man to an exalted and happy state. To exhibit this part of the subject fully would occupy far more time and room than are now allowed us. We can only suggest the material points, and this in the fewest words.

What then are, let us inquire, the elements of moral power demanded in an agency, that it may effectually reach the case in which mankind are found?

To present the matter in the simplest possible way, we answer—that the things required in order to the recovery of sinful men are GRACE, LOVE, and the SPIRITUAL ENERGY which shall give these their appropriate influence on the heart. In other words, the instrumentality which would restore sinful humanity to peace, and purity, and elevated life, must be able first to relieve the conscience from the burden of guilt which past transgressions have imposed, and then to draw its affections toward holiness and make them to centre on God as the infinitely Holy. It must assure of full release from the curse of sin which rests upon the soul, and of complete and final rescue from the slavery of sin in which it is involved.

We say, then, that the gospel of Jesus Christ does come to the heart of man in all the power of free and abounding *grace.* It comes, that is, with the full and specific offer of unqualified forgiveness on the part of God for past iniquities. It has always been just here that all mere human devices for the elevation of the world have revealed their worthlessness. They could not meet the soul's first want. They could not utter a word, with any certainty, as to whether there could be any such thing as pardon for transgression. But go to human beings where and when you will, and speak to them of God and duty, and the moment you can gain attention and can bring home to the mind a clear conviction of the obligation of God's law, that moment you find a burden on the conscience that presses like a millstone. "Oh, my sins! my sins! I feel that they deserve a heavy judgment. They cover me with shame and fill me with foreboding. God is pure—infinitely pure; I dare not even lift up my eyes to him, for the overpowering splendour of his holiness flashes on the darkness of my soul like a devouring fire! What shall I do? Whither shall I fly? I deserve the displeasure of the eternally Good whom I have so causelessly abused! This weight upon my heart must crush me, for I cannot roll it off!" Such, for substance, is the language of every awakened conscience. Will you offer to such a man an ingenious speculation, a plausible conjecture, the performance of a penance or a ceremony, an outward reformation, or any similar expedient, as a relief? You may as well propose to amuse with idle tales the wretch that writhes upon a bed of torture. But, hark! the word "FORGIVENESS!" "God can and will forgive the penitent!" proclaims the gospel. "Can he? Will he?" cries the oppressed, despairing soul. "Glad tidings! glad tidings!—then there is hope—there is hope for me!" And when he is pointed to Christ crucified, to an atoning Saviour, to the Lamb of God that taketh away the sin of the world, his soul is stirred to its lowest depths to find that his first great want—that of deliverance from merited condemnation—is, by the *grace* which the gospel offers him, most fully met.

But the work of entire recovery is as yet but half

accomplished. Let the Ethiopian change his skin and the leopard his spots, then may they also who are accustomed to do evil learn to do well. The power of disordered appetite and inclination is a mighty power. The chains of sinful habit are like chains of triple brass. The apathy of blunted moral feeling is like the drowsiness of a Lethean stupor. The law of sin, in the members, brings the whole man into captivity to the power of sin. In addition to forgiveness, therefore, the case of the sinful soul demands something which can evolve within a moral force, a vital spring of action which shall have energy enough to conquer fixed propensity and lawless passion, to wake into activity the moral affections and change their habitual current,—in a word, to emancipate the moral man.

Just what the case requires the gospel offers. It presents, in objective facts, to the understanding and the heart the riches of an infinite love in God, and reveals the certainty of an inward subjective ministry of the Divine Spirit for the renovation of the soul. The gospel, whereever it goes, at once makes known, and is attended by, a special vitalizing spiritual influence, which is to the obdurate, unfeeling heart on which it falls what the sunshine and the genial showers are to the cold, hard, barren earth —a softening, life-producing agency. Then it exhibits *God himself as stooping to redeem!* That very Being against whom sin has been committed it reveals as full of compassion towards the sinner—so full of pure, paternal, yes, more than paternal love, that since he might not otherwise fitly spare the sinner, he spared not his own Son, but gave him freely for the world, that whosoever should believe on him might have eternal life. It presents that Son as voluntarily leaving the glory which he had with the Father before the world was; as being made flesh; as descending to the condition of a servant; as being despised and rejected of men; as enduring inward agony beyond description in the garden, although himself sinless and pure; as making his soul an offering for sin, the one sacrifice, of which all Jewish victims were but types,—or as he himself expressed it, as shedding his blood for many for the remission of sins. It makes known the Father as receiving, through the mediation of the Son, all, even the chief of sinners, who believe in and accept him, into the estate and privileges of his holy family, and to the heirship of his eternal love and blessing.

This, then, is the wonderful economy of man's redemption, as devised and executed by that very goodness which human sin has dishonoured and abused. These are the heights and depths of a love towards the guilty which is immeasurable and infinite. The inflexibleness of eternal justice, and the yearning of eternal mercy, are together unfolded to rebellious men. Whatever is grand and awful in unbending devotion to the right—whatever is sweet and winning in benevolence that is spontaneous and pure—whatever is admirable in condescension—whatever is touching in suffering borne by a free self-sacrifice for the sake of the undeserving—whatever is lovely and noble in the goodness that receives and embraces the guilty who are penitent,—God in Christ exhibits to the world in the simple yet stupendous facts which constitute the gospel. When these facts, by the power of the Divine Spirit, are so effectually set home on the hearts of sinful men that they are seen and felt in somewhat of their proper force and import, the rocky heart is melted into tenderness, the resisting will is finally subdued, the power of sin is broken, and there is opened a fountain in the deep recesses of the soul, from which thenceforward there gushes up a tide of holy love to God, and to all that is truly excellent and pure. This is the living water, of which the Saviour said, it shall be in the soul a well of water springing up into everlasting life. It is, in fact, a new, spiritual, progressive, and immortal life begun—a life that has energy enough to raise up from its ruins man's originally God-like nature, to adorn it with every moral grace and virtue, and restore it to its pristine glory. Such power is in the cross of Christ. Such is the moral efficacy of that gospel, the sum and substance of which is Christ crucified—a revelation of grace, and love, and regenerating power. Neither subjectively nor objectively is any provision needful to mankind, in their state of sin and suffering, that the gospel does not bring them.

If scepticism denies what it has been our purpose to maintain, we have only to appeal to undeniable facts in the history of Christianity. We have already seen that every human device has failed to recover mankind from the debasement and misery of sin. But has the gospel failed in a single instance in which it has been fairly tried? Where is the individual, where is the community, or the nation, that has practically received the Christian religion, that has not been elevated, and made virtuous and happy exactly in proportion to the thoroughness and cordiality of the reception? Where are now found, in all the world, the highest excellences of private character, the best discharge of social duties, the greatest amount of public order, intelligence, and virtue, the largest measure, in short, of everything that charms and adorns existence here, or qualifies for higher scenes of being—where but in those favoured places in which the simple truths of uncorrupted Christianity are most impressed on the minds of men? It cannot be denied that evangelical truth has made the world to bloom wherever it has found a way. It has made good men and great men without number. It has filled millions, in every walk in life, with a calm and abiding peace, in spite of all the storms, and wrestlings, and sorrows that belong to an evil world; and has sent them, victors over death, to people the eternal paradise of God. The experience of all time declares the essential gospel of Jesus Christ to be universally the power of God unto salvation to every one that believeth. It is, therefore, to be distinctly recognised and used as the sole hope of a fallen world.

Whoever, then, is the enemy of genuine Christianity is, it is plain, the enemy of mankind. Whoever attempts to weaken its authority or obstruct its progress among men, not only assails the best hopes, the highest welfare of the world's future, but does what in him lies to consign that future to wretchedness and guilt without relief. The ever-renewed attempts to overthrow the religion of the New Testament, whether originating in pride of intellect, in the blindness of an unbelieving heart, or in direct and conscious hostility to truth and goodness, are all indeed futile. The truth of God will ever stand, as it has stood, unshaken, to the confusion of those that war against it. But such will reveal themselves as the foes of human happiness, as wanting the spirit of God's kingdom, and as, whether intentionally or not, the allies of the prince of darkness. Who would not shrink from assuming this position?

If, then, you hold the welfare of the world as dear—if you would wish to put an end to the groans which, through the ages past, it has been sending up to heaven—if you would desire that the day of which prophets have foretold such glorious things may come, when joy and gladness, as the fruit of purity and love, of order, freedom, and general intelligence and piety, shall reign through all the earth—if you would be yourselves benefactors of your species, while exalted and made happy in your own persons, accept heartily and practically the gospel as it is, in its simple yet momentous facts, and do your utmost while you live to bring others to feel its blessed power.

> "'Tis Revelation satisfies all doubts,
> Explains all mysteries except her own,
> And so illuminates the path of life,
> That fools discover it, and stray no more.
> Now tell me, dignified and sapient sir,
> My man of morals, nurtured in the shades
> Of Academus—is this false or true?
> Is Christ the abler teacher, or the schools?
> If Christ, then why resort at every turn
> To Athens, or to Rome, for wisdom short
> Of man's occasions, when in Him reside
> Grace, knowledge, comfort—an unfathomed store?"

Yes, it is time, indeed, to abandon the poor folly of

seeking in the wisdom and the power of man what is only to be found in the wisdom and the power of God in Jesus Christ—relief from the guilt that crushes and enslaves humanity, and from the woes, individual and social, temporal and eternal, which sin has made the sad inheritance of our self-ruined race. Christ is the Light of the world, and in him is the Life of men. His gospel is the world's sole hope.

XIV.

God to be chosen as a Guide.

JER. iii. 4: "*Wilt thou not from this time cry unto me, My Father, thou art the guide of my youth?*"

THE period of youth, consider it in whatever light we will, is full of interest. It is the period of comparative freedom from the contaminations of an evil world. It is the season of happy impulses, of glowing hopes, of high aspirations, of sincere and warm affections, of free and generous confidence, and, in general, of the virtues that are most lovely and the manners that are most engaging. It is also the morning of life's day—the still lake out of which issues its rushing stream—the gate-way to its arena—the seed-time for its harvests of good or ill. To all who have come to know by experience what life actually is, and who have seriously pondered its vast and solemn responsibilities, a group of young persons just advancing to maturity is one of the most interesting sights to be met with in the world.

It is especially so to the true minister of Christ. He watches for the souls of all, as one that must give an account. But he sees in those who are on the threshold of active life the opening buds of the garden which he has it in charge to cultivate and keep. He comprehends their relation to the future, and from his peculiar position he has a clearer and more impressive view than most others are likely to have of their special circumstances and their perils. As he stands upon his watch-tower, and sees them with cheerful looks and hopeful spirits coming forward to meet life's inevitable toils and dangers, he is like one who, posted on some headland, looks abroad on a new and well-rigged fleet, that, with snowy canvas and streamers sporting with the wind, freighted with precious treasures and manned with noble hearts, is just issuing from the port and putting forth on the stormy sea. It is impossible for such a person not to look onward from this fair array to the scene which will present itself when the howling tempest has done its desolating work. Many a good ship will then lie an unsightly wreck, many a one will have gone down into the unknown deep, some will have been left crippled and scarcely better than destroyed, and only a few of the whole number will have safely weathered the fearful buffetings, and accomplished the objects of the voyage. Or the Christian pastor, while he surveys the youth around him, may be likened to an officer who is marshalling the young and brave, and preparing them, by proper discipline, to go forth to the contests of the field. Such a one looks now only on freshness, strength, and beauty. He admires the light and graceful movement, the well-adjusted trappings, and more than all, the lofty ardour of his band. But then he looks forward, with prophetic glance, to the day succeeding battle. He sees only a remnant of all his goodly company escaped safe from the deadly struggle. Many have fallen in the carnage and have perished. Many are wounded to linger on and die.

Many will live only to suffer all their days from the loss of limbs, or other enduring injuries. Can it be otherwise than that when the watchman for souls sees those of his charge who are yet in early years just putting forth on life's eventful sea, or, according to the other illustration, just girding on the harness for the great life-battle through which they are to pass, he should regard them with a yearning heart, and should offer for them his earnest prayers, and give to them such counsels as his own experience and observation, and more especially the word of God, suggest?

It is, my younger friends, with deep interest that I think of you, and look on you from week to week. For you, with sincerity I hope, I do habitually bow the knee to the Father of all mercies, beseeching him to bless and save you; and to you, to you in a special manner, I bring his gracious message. The great God, your Father and my Father, in his super-abounding goodness, does virtually address each of you in the language of the text. You may rightly take, as if addressed immediately to you, this touching appeal to Israel of old,—"Wilt thou not from this time cry unto me, My Father, thou art the guide of my youth?" I would, if possible, assist you to decide the question thus proposed. In doing this, I will ask you to consider the need in which you stand of guidance, the wisdom of making God your guide, and the fitness of the present as the time in which to receive him in that character.

I say then, first of all, that you do greatly need *some* aithful and effective guidance in the shaping of your lives.

The need is at once obvious and pressing. It rests upon so many grounds, that in any attempt to state them, the only difficulty lies in being brief. Some of them, however, I will notice.

You need such guidance because the path of duty and of safety is often exceedingly difficult to find. The great principles on which every person is bound to act in the ordering of his life, are indeed well settled. They are authoritatively delivered in the Scriptures, are assented to by reason and conscience, and have been confirmed and illustrated by experience. The principles to which I here refer are the general principles of moral duty—as, for example, that we should acknowledge the existence and perfection of God; that we should love him first and best of all, and our neighbours as ourselves; together with the common laws of prudence,—such as that intelligence, industry, economy, forethought, and the like, are necessary conditions of success, and of safety and happiness in living. In respect to these there need be no perplexity. But with you, as capable of reflection, of judgment, and of choice, is left the responsibility of making the application of these principles in all the practical details of life. In every important step, almost at every hour of every day, you are obliged to raise the questions—Is this right? Is this wrong? Is this true? Is this expedient? Is this safe?—and then immediately to decide and act on your decision. Often when determining what you are bound to accept as duty or to receive as truth, you have many circumstances to consider, many probabilities to estimate, many opposing arguments to weigh. You are aware that the most trifling actions, or those that seem such, are often followed by most momentous consequences, and so you are at a loss to know how much importance to attach to what you do. In short, while the general direction in which you are to move, if you intend to live wisely, is obvious enough, you may still find perplexities at every point, to extricate yourselves from which will try, perhaps even baffle, your utmost wisdom. The wrong ways are a thousand, the right way is but one. The wrong looks often like the right, the right often like the wrong. Who is sufficient for these things? Who of you can trust himself,—can venture to take his way unaided through all the mazes of the labyrinth of life, to shape his own course, amidst treacherous shoals and hidden rocks, across the mighty sea? You cannot seriously consider the difficulty you must find in determining your way without perceiving clearly that you need effectual guidance.

You need such guidance, also, because your own strong impulses are likely to mislead you. We had occasion in a preceding discourse, and in another connection, to notice the fact that the natural appetites and passions, and the desires and propensities which choice and habit have created, may exert a very great influence on the judgment. This is true, not only in deciding between truth and falsehood, but as well in deciding between right and wrong. It is easy to believe that to be right or useful which accords with inclination. It is hard to think that to be obligatory, or best, to which the feelings are averse, and which involves the necessity of painful self-denial. Let two paths lie before the weary traveller, the one of which leads smoothly along the plain, while the other climbs the rugged steep, and he is strongly predisposed to believe the more agreeable the right.

Now, although it is certainly true, in an important sense that Wisdom's ways are pleasantness, and all her paths are peace, it is by no means true that all her ways are agreeable to present inclination, or the bent of the sinful heart. You will find often that appetite and passion will plead against the plain and positive demands of duty; and it will require a strong resistance to overcome this pleading and to make a choice against all selfish impulses, in obedience to conscience. How great, then, the embarrassment which the desire of self-indulgence must many times occasion, when duty is not plain, but doubtful, and you have it to determine! How easily, in such circumstances, may the impulses of feeling pervert the understanding, and so make the worse appear the better reason as to lead you utterly astray! Is it not nearly certain, since you form your decisions in the affairs of every day under such misleading influences, that without *some* wise guidance you will be drawn aside from duty and from peace; that you will be led into the pursuit of some of the thousand phantoms,

> "That lead to bewilder, and dazzle to blind"—

and which, after dancing for a while before the eye, on a sudden grow dim and disappear? Such a result would seem to be inevitable.

Still further, you need guidance in the shaping of your lives, because there are many who will studiously seek your ruin. It is hard always to make the young believe this; yet sooner or later experience brings conviction of the fact. There are found even in the best conditions of society the openly debased and vicious. They have broken away from moral restraint and disowned the authority of conscience. They have given full dominion to appetite and lust. Like the master whom they have given themselves to serve, they have said in their hearts—

"Evil, be thou my good;"

and like him, they go about continually seeking whom they may devour. Having learned to be unscrupulously immoral, or even impious, and unblushingly to glory in their shame, they are ready to make others as shameless as themselves: not that they boldly avow this as their object,—if they did this, the danger were comparatively small,—but by their spirit and example, they first taint the moral atmosphere around those whom they are desirous to corrupt, and then gradually draw them, by one artifice and another, down to their own pollution.

Besides the grossly wicked, there are many others who will seek to reach you with influences fitted to destroy your virtuous sentiments, and principles, and your ultimate well-being. There are many not openly corrupt, who are utterly corrupt in heart. While they exhibit, perhaps, respectable outward morals, this class of persons will either distinctly advocate, or covertly let fall, the most loose and pernicious maxims and opinions. If possible, they will infuse into your minds their own dreary scepticism, their light estimate of serious things, and especially their contempt for the piety and conscientiousness of decidedly religious men. By such methods, though retaining themselves some outward show of respect for goodness, they will try to sap all the foundations of goodness in your heart. It is difficult to say which is the more dangerous to encounter—those who are unblushingly wicked in their lives, or those whose depravity is artful and concealed.

Through such enemies to your virtue and peace, and others which need not be particularly described, you have to make your way. To avoid them is impossible. To escape their influence and to elude their artifices is often extremely difficult. When least suspecting danger, your feet may be entangled in their net. Oh, who that comprehends how much he has at stake, can help trembling, when he thinks that so many and such deadly foes beset all the path of life he is to tread! Can any young person, who seriously reflects on his position, doubt that he greatly needs some friendly direction on his way? If, then, we also add the great revealed truth, that the prince and powers of darkness are likewise ever watching to allure your feet into the ways of death, new grounds of apprehension are supplied which make the need to appear more urgent still.

I will only mention further, that your need of guidance is strongly set forth in the melancholy fact that so many are continually ruined. Where many fall, there is reason that all should fear. Look, then, at facts, which are offered on all sides to your notice, in illustration of the perils that beset you. Or if you will take a wider view, apply to those whose opportunities and experience have been greater than your own. Go to some man now past the meridian of life, whose character and habits, with the divine blessing, have made him honoured and successful. He was one of a band, more or less numerous, who set out in life together. They came forth from their homes and from the schoolroom differing, perhaps, but little either in their talents or acquirements. Ask him to tell you where those his early associates are now, and what he remembers of their history. Ah! how painful the recollection and the recital! One, he will say, as he brings back the half-forgotten past, looked on the wine when it was red, and he went early to the drunkard's grave. Another yielded to the love of vain display; and after a brief career of brilliant folly and extravagance, he passed by bankruptcy to poverty, and was soon forgotten by the world. A third indulged, at first, in some trifling dishonesty, and then was led on till he became a villain, and finally went to prison, or to an ignominious death. A fourth gave loose to sensual appetite; and then from impurity of thought and word, he went on step by step, till he suffered the miseries, and met at last the fate of the worn-out profligate. A fifth was taken in the gambler's snare, and fell by suicide. A sixth—but why should I go on? So daily perish, on life's broad arena, the hopes of fathers and of mothers! So sink into the depths of shame and ruin many who should have shone as brilliant stars in the galaxy of intellect—should have found a place among the noblest spirits that have ever done honour to humanity and climbed the enviable heights of fair renown. The road-side of life is all whitened with the bones of the multitudes who have fallen thus, having made, by their own missteps, an utter wreck of their hopes, their characters, and their all. With such evidence of the perils of your future, can you doubt your need of some friendly hand to lead you?

Let us pass on, then, in the second place, to insist on the reasonableness, the wisdom of making God your guide. On this part of the subject I must be comparatively brief. A thousand reasons might easily be mentioned why every young person, whatever may be his particular position, should look up with a filial spirit unto God, and cry, "My Father, THOU art the guide of my youth." I must content myself, however, with two which seem to be the chief, and which may in some sort comprehend the rest, or at least suggest them.

The first is, that *you owe it to God himself* thus to honour him with your confidence. It is his right to expect it of you. That your hearts should be directed towards him, that you should recognise him as the Fountain of all wisdom, as the providential Director of events, as the Father of your spirits, and the benevolent Guardian of your welfare, and should commit yourselves to the leading of his will,—all necessarily results from the fact that he is what he is, God over all, the perfection of being, the essence and centre of all goodness. Since he is such a Being, he is in the highest degree competent to guide you. He most perfectly understands the constitution of your nature, for he made it what it is. He knows every spring of thought, feeling, and desire, and every avenue by which either good or evil influence can find access to your heart. When the line of duty is obscure and you are troubled in spirit with perplexity and doubt, he can make light to break in upon you as when the morning dawns in beauty upon the night. When passion is restless and clamours for indulgence, he can so breathe his Spirit on you, as to hush all the tumult of the soul to peace. When wicked men and wicked spirits are watching around you with intent to destroy you, if they can, he can put over you the shield of his almightiness, and defend you from every device by which they would work you ill. Thus qualified to afford you the very guidance that you need, when out of pure good-will to you he condescends to offer it, can it be doubtful whether it is due to him that you should gratefully accept the offer? Not to do it is to treat him with dishonour. That you have not done it hitherto, if indeed you have failed to do it, has given him reason to say in reference to you, as he said in respect to Israel by the prophet, "If I then be a Father, where is now mine honour?"

The second reason which ought to determine you to take God to be your guide is this, that God alone can afford you a *sufficient* guidance. That he is able to grant you an effectual safe-conduct, has just now been observed. But where can you find another to whose care and leading you can safely and without anxiety commit the infinitely precious interests of your being? Do you think of parents? Have you a parent who is wise enough and strong enough to guide and keep you in all the emergencies of life, and who is also omnipresent? Will you choose your favourite teacher, or the moralist, or the philosopher you most admire? Believe it, you will find when the hour of trial comes, that you can as soon light up black midnight with a taper, or defend yourselves against wild beasts with straws, as solve your gloomy doubts and make your safety sure by any such assistance. Will you rely on your own reason to conduct you? And so did thousands who now groan beneath the hopeless wreck of ruined happiness and ruined souls! No, no, my youthful friends; neither will any human wisdom, nor any human aid, be found equal to your need. Learn all you can from the counsels of wise parents. Despise not the teachings of the schools, nor the lessons of true philosophy. Develop your own reason and listen to its voice. But trust in none of these as your grand reliance. God alone can be your sufficient guide.

It only remains, therefore, in the third place, to consider the question of time. When should God's offered guidance be accepted? May it be accepted now? We wish to insist on the fitness of securing it at once. "Wilt thou not *from this time* cry unto me?" Such is the divine demand.

The fact that the present is a *practicable* time—a time in which, without hindrance, God may be intelligently and cordially accepted as a guide—is in itself a proof that it is a *proper* time. If you are ever to enjoy God's guidance —ever to have him lead you through the trials and the perils of the wilderness of life, it must be by your own deliberate and hearty act. At some specific time you must cry to him for the purpose of expressing your desire. Humbly, earnestly, and as one that cannot do without it, you must ask at his hands the blessing which you want. What, then, is there to forbid the immediate presentation of your suit? You are now in the enjoyment of health and reason, with nothing to prevent you from attending to the matter intelligently and calmly. On the part of God there is nothing to hinder your free approach to the mercy-seat, and nothing to shut out your request. Around you is the holy stillness of the Sabbath, and all the sweet and sacred influences of the Christian sanctuary; so that if you are really disposed to take your gracious Father as your guide in this auspicious hour, there is nothing to oppose. You may now secure this inestimable good. This hour of grace is therefore a fit, because a most favourable time.

Still further, the *present* time is the very time that God himself proposes: "Remember *now* thy Creator." So everywhere throughout the Scriptures. It is always in the present, and never in the future, that he issues his commands and holds out his invitations. This makes your duty plain. Suppose that some person of distinction had proposed to grant you a great favour, to receive which you were to call on him at his dwelling. If he had specified no time at which you should present yourself, you might naturally feel solicitude lest you should disoblige him by calling at an inconvenient hour. But he himself has precisely fixed the time. Then surely you can feel no embarrassment whatever. No hour can be so suitable as that which he has named. The case is just the same in the matter now before us. In offering himself to you, as a kind, a faithful, and an all-sufficient guide, the Father of all mercy is pleased to name the time in which you may accept the benefit. What other time, let me demand of you, can be so fit as this present passing hour which he has specified? "Wilt thou not from this time cry unto me?"

But this is not all. It is at this present time that your need of the blessing in question is becoming manifest and urgent. The difficulties and the dangers that create the need are not remote, but are now actually at hand. If it is true that they are likely to thicken as you go forward, it is true also that they are already numerous and formidable enough. Plainly it is here, at the very opening of life's great and momentous scene, at that stand-point from which there are so many divergent paths, that it is especially fit that you should choose your guide. You want now his friendly offices, that you may not start wrong in the race. You want them now, that you may not waste in bewilderment and error the choicest, freshest, palmiest days of your existence, or, stumbling at the outset, be precipitated to an untimely and fatal fall. Is it not preeminently fit that you should now take hold of God's conducting hand, since it is at this time that it will be most signally a blessing to you to be directed by it?

Finally, the fact that the present may not improbably be the only time in which you will have it in your power to secure the divine guidance, affords yet another illustration of the fitness of the opportunity now afforded. You remember what the Scriptures say of those who have rejected God's advances: "Because I have called, and ye refused; I have stretched out my hand, and no man regarded; but ye have set at nought all my counsel, and would none of my reproof: I also will laugh at your calamity; I will mock when your fear cometh; when your fear cometh as desolation, and your destruction cometh as a whirlwind; when distress and anguish come upon you:

then shall ye call upon me, but I will not answer; ye shall seek me early, but ye shall not find me; for that ye hated instruction, and did not choose the fear of the Lord." Appalling words! A very brief period, you who are now in the freshness and blossom of your youth, may bring important changes in God's mode of dealing with you. It may cut you off from the Christian privileges you now enjoy. It may, by some visitation of divine Providence which it shall bring, so disturb and agitate your mind with cares or sufferings, as to render you incapable of cool reflection. It may place you in circumstances in which it shall be morally impossible for you to make God your friend, and to secure his protecting care. In a word, if you do not accept the present call of God, and respond with a sincere and earnest heart, "My Father, thou art the guide of my youth," it is highly probable that many of you at least will never ask his guidance till too late; and for the want of it will go astray, as so many have done before you, and miserably perish. Oh, is not this most eminently the fitting time for the final turning of your soul to God, in the recognition of him as your only sufficient guide?

Will you listen, then, to God's gracious call at once? Through the great sacrifice of Calvary, the dying love of Jesus, you may become a child of God to-day, a holy, happy child, if you have not been one before. These hours of youth are flying, flying swiftly, like vapours driven by the wind. Onward—onward to all that is serious in life, in death, and in the eternity beyond, you are hastening rapidly, with the steady march of time.

The question what shall be your characters and destiny will soon be unalterably settled. *Shall it be settled well?* Would that I had the power to lay this solemn question, in all its proper weight, upon each of your souls! Would that I had the power to uncover in your sight the perils that shall certainly attend your every step in life; and then that I might rend before your eyes the mighty veil that now conceals the secrets of that tremendous future down whose interminable ages each soul for itself is ere long to begin its flight! Then you might see how blessed and glorious you *may* be, if you will but at once submit yourselves to the kind leadings of Eternal Love; and how fallen, ruined, and unalterably wretched you *must* be, if you reject God's guidance, and so are lost to good. At least you will bear me witness, when you and I shall meet,—as meet we shall before God's great tribunal,—if it be found that, refusing to take his guidance, you were hopelessly undone, that you perished not unwarned, not without being tenderly entreated to accept the proffered guidance of that compassionate and loving Father who had it in his heart to receive you as a child, and to love and bless you evermore. "The fear of the Lord, that is wisdom; and to depart from evil, that is understanding."

XV.

The Value of a Life as related to our Time.

LUKE x. 23, 24: "*And he turned him unto his disciples, and said privately, Blessed are the eyes which see the things that ye see: for I tell you, that many prophets and kings have desired to see those things which ye see, and have not seen them; and to hear those things which ye hear, and have not heard them.*"

WHAT our blessed Lord wished his disciples to understand when he addressed to them these words was this,—that they ought to esteem it a great advantage to live in his time, to hear his words, and to see his mighty works. As compared with the ages in which the kings and prophets lived, who had predicted, and longed to see, the day when the Messiah, the Hope of Israel, should come, the era in which Christ appeared and exercised his ministry among men was as the sunrise to the glimmer of early dawn,—an era of pre-eminent light and opportunity, in which, rightly understood, it was indeed an inestimable privilege to live. Taken in this view, the text naturally suggests the thought that the value of any human life depends essentially on the circumstances under which that life is to be lived. It is for the sake of this thought that I have called your attention to the passage. Nothing better occurs to me than to address you, as appropriate to this occasion, on the *value of a life*, as estimated in relation to this our time, and to the present condition of the world.

Let the subject be distinctly understood. The value of any individual life, in given circumstances, will of course depend on the amount of natural capacity possessed, on the end proposed in living, and on the length to which the life extends. But it is not of these things that I desire to speak. I wish to take just the opposite view. I wish to show that, with a given capacity, a given rectitude of purpose, and a given length of days, the value of a life in the present state of things, as regards ourselves, is vastly greater than it could have been at any former period of the world.

Another word of explanation before proceeding with the subject. The *value* of a life. To whom? I shall perhaps be asked. To the individual himself; or to the world and the universe? *Both*, it may be answered;—its intrinsic value in all its relations and results. The value of a life is proportioned to what is accomplished by it in the broadest possible estimate.

What I have to show, then, in order to illustrate the truth derived from the text is, that, in respect to all the chief circumstances on which the value of a life must depend, our time has a vast superiority over all past periods of the world.

I say then, first of all, that in no past age of the world have such means of individual development existed as are now enjoyed by us.

As to the early intellectual and social condition of the Oriental nations, with the exception of the Hebrews, we know comparatively little. That of the Egyptians is involved in similar obscurity. No doubt that in the countries of the further East, in Media and in Persia, and also on the Nile, there was, at an early period, a very considerable amount of a certain kind of intellectual culture. There is ample evidence, however, that it was narrow in its range, and confined to a particular class, or classes, including but a small portion of the people. Among the Greeks, education in art, letters, and philosophy, was certainly carried to a high degree of refinement; and the Romans, on the basis of Grecian learning, wrought out for their time a splendid literature. But neither among the Greeks nor the Romans was knowledge widely diffused: the facilities for education were not accessible to the masses; and while philosophers speculated acutely, both in the Old and the New Academy, and statesmen, orators, historians, and poets appeared in illustrious succession, it was nevertheless true that, for by far the greater portion of the population, the means of individual culture were very limited indeed. Without the printing press the dissemination of thought was difficult and slow.

Since the revival of learning in modern times, there has undoubtedly been a steadily advancing extension of knowledge and education among the western nations. Italy, Germany, England, and France, have had their golden periods of intellectual development, the result of which has been works in the various departments of letters and science, which are not likely to perish so long as the world shall stand. But if we look, for example, at the condition of the great body of the Italian people in the best days of the Medici; or of the German people in the time of Frederick the Great, or of Luther; or at that of the

English people in the reign of Queen Elizabeth, or even of Queen Anne; or at that of the French people in the days of Louis XIV., it is plain that, in respect to the means of education, in the common meaning of the term, and still more in respect to other influences which tend to make every man a man, those periods were far behind the present century. The difference in favour of the present is greater, in fact, than we find it easy to believe.

We need not speak of the present state of other countries. It will be sufficient for our purpose to confine our attention to our own; and when we assert that never before, since the world began, did any entire people enjoy such means of individual development as we are enjoying now and here, the only difficulty in substantiating the assertion lies in the abundance of the proof at hand. For what are the means by which individual life is awakened, stimulated, and matured into healthful vigour? Are schools essential? But when and where were schools of every grade, from the nursery to the university, brought so completely within the reach of all who are willing to receive their benefits, as among ourselves to-day? Are the products of the press effective to the end? But was any people ever so completely deluged with newspapers, magazines, and quarterlies, with children's books, school books, books in every department of literature and science, of philosophy and religion; books of all prices, of all sizes, and on all conceivable subjects? Are words spoken by living lips adapted to quicken individual souls and elicit their hidden forces? Did ever a land resound from end to end and through all its deep recesses as does this, with harangues of all imaginable sorts—lectures, speeches, sermons, debates, forensic arguments and scholarly orations? Is individual mind aroused and excited by the general spirit of society, the atmosphere of intellectual and moral life by which it is surrounded? Where was there ever such an intensity of social energy—such vehemence of thought and purpose, such burning, restless eagerness of soul—as we see glowing in all eyes, and breathing through all the activities of the social system, in this our time and country? And lastly, does Christianity, with her disclosures of man's personal responsibility and the grandeur of his being as related to God and immortality, with her holy inspirations, and her manifold vitalizing influences, act powerfully on individual man for his exaltation? Where, then, or at what other time, has Christianity been brought to bear so widely, and directly, and with so little to obstruct her healthful action, on the hearts and lives of men, as in all the older portions of our land, where, as an all-pervading force, she exerts a moulding influence alike on institutions and on people? We are not saying that any or all these means of individual development are producing all the results to be desired; or that in the matter of profiting by them, we have not many things to learn. We may have been, we may still be bad scholars, however good the school. But it is undeniable that the means themselves are such as were never enjoyed to an equal extent before. If there is not among us, as a people, more individuality—more force of personal character, intellectual and moral—or to say the whole in short, more real manhood and womanhood than have been found in other centuries, it can only be because we have not understood our birthright, and have failed to make the best use of our advantages. What is the truth on this point we will not now inquire. Enough that there is everything in our position that would seem necessary to bring out whatever may be in us, and to make the most of all our capabilities. So far as the value of a life depends on the means of individual development, it was *never* so great as now.

I come then to say further, as a second thing, that never before did any people enjoy such liberty and scope of useful action as our time is now affording us.

I do not here refer to our civil and religious freedom, except as these are the necessary conditions of all activity. It is to the multitudinous openings for useful and honourable action, the unequalled number and variety of proffered opportunities, that I have special reference. In no age has the restlessness of man failed to express itself in one way or another. But it has to a great extent been true in former centuries that few paths comparatively, leading to good and noble ends, have been open to the larger portion of society. In Babylon and Nineveh, in Egypt, in Greece and Rome, in the feudal ages of Europe, not only was there a lack of the means to produce a high degree of individual development, but what of such development there actually was, could not express itself in appropriate activities ; in part from the checks and hindrances imposed by despotic governments, and in part because the opening of the manifold channels of industry and enterprise is a work pertaining to a higher state of civilization than had then been reached. Not having open to it ways of good and wholesome effort, the force of society, by a sort of necessity, then expended itself in civil contests, in fierce and bloody wars, or in chimerical and fruitless undertakings, like the Crusades. In proportion as European civilization has advanced, there has been more of individual liberty and an increase of facilities for individual action there; but within the present century there has been an advance beyond anything before conceived, and more among ourselves than anywhere else—not even excepting England, which in all healthful progress is at the head of the Old World.

Look a moment at the facts. There is no check to the liberty of individual action on the part of the government under which we live, except simply what is demanded as a condition of social order. What that is right, and honourable, and good, is not every member of society free to do to the full measure of his capacity? And then what *prizes*—of wealth, of social happiness, of knowledge, of fame, of station, and of power, are not within the reach of even the most humble? What sort of talent is there to which there is not open some good and inviting field? Will a man till the ground? He is enabled now by science and mechanical skill to do it in the most productive manner and with the least expenditure of labour? Will a man engage in trade? What is there that is not made an article of traffic, from the very stones and the hills of sand and pebbles, up to the richest products of nature and of art; and whither can one look, over lands or seas, to the four winds of heaven, that he shall not see the beaten paths of commerce right before him, inviting him to try his fortune if he will? Will a man speak? There are thousands of listening ears awaiting him. Will he write? Millions of hungry readers are ready to devour every worthy product of his pen. Will he be a statesman? No hamlet in the land is so remote that his sayings and doings shall not be known and debated there. Will any one live in seclusion and give himself to thought? Electric wires and thundering trains will bring him incessant stimulants to thinking, and will enable him to transmit his thoughts to others, if he will, before they have had time to cool. Will one devote himself to philanthropic labours? He will neither want materials to work upon, nor sympathy and co-operation in his efforts. Will he rise to the height of Christian heroism, and, inspired with faith and love, attempt self-sacrificing toils in the dissemination of the Christian faith? He will find himself united with vast multitudes of kindred spirit, and will easily put himself in connection with remotest regions of the world. I need not pursue this course of illustration. To every one of us there is given, by the time and place in which we live, a liberty for every sort of action, an extent and scope of influence impossible to any age preceding, and such as the men of other generations could never even have imagined. The reality is beyond their dreams. If the end of life is useful action, when were there such facilities as at this day?

Still further, it may be added, as a third fact in relation to our time, that never so much as now was right individual effort effective for great results. All ages have had those who, in comparison with others of their time, have done great things, and have left enduring marks of their power upon the world. But how many of the best and wisest of other times have laboured all their lives to accomplish some noble purpose, for which their age was not prepared, or in the way of which the existing state of things arrayed a thousand difficulties! How many of the choicest and most gifted spirits of our race have sown in tears, through years of patient toil, the seed of blessings not by any possibility to be reaped till long after they were dead! The memories of such are fragrant through the ages. They are God's jewels, that have gleamed out often amidst surrounding rubbish. If there is any sight more noble than all others in this world, it is that of men or women expending their best energies upon some work of love, with their eyes fixed only on those who shall live when they have lain down, perhaps long, in the silent dust. This is pre-eminently the God-like in well-doing—the sublime spectacle of disinterested goodness.

But after all, it is certainly to be regarded as a thing to be desired, to be ourselves permitted to reap, at least to *begin* to reap, where we have sown. It is a happiness to be placed in a position in which the ruling forces around us appear to be working with us, and not against us; to see that the course of divine Providence, the currents of human thought and opinion, and the general movements of society, combine to give effect to our right endeavours, whatever their specific character may be. It is certainly a most natural and reasonable desire, that our well-directed efforts may be attended not only with the largest, but with the speediest possible results.

Now, I am very far from saying that there are no difficulties to be encountered in our time by those who strive to accomplish something worthy in their lives. There are now, and probably always will be, difficulties not only to be met, but to be strenuously wrestled with, in doing good in this evil world. The ample and unprecedented facilities for doing almost anything to which we have referred, by no means presuppose the absence of opposing influences. Labour itself is irksome; and by a law of our condition, as fixed by divine Providence, no considerable good can be attained without effort made with some degree of self-denial, and in opposition to some things which will test courage, energy, and patience. There would be no room for great and heroic conduct if such were not the case.

But when I say that at no time before was individual effort so effective, so sure to be fruitful, and that speedily, of good results, I would have the following things considered :—

First, that along with means of individual development, and liberty and scope of action, there is in the world at large—in the more enlightened portion of mankind—a greatly increased susceptibility to new and right impressions. There is far less of *inertia*, in man and in society, to be overcome, in the introduction of any new truth, the giving of any new impulse, the setting in motion of any new enterprise that can be shown to be at once possible and useful, than there ever was before. The rapid progress of art, science, intercommunication, and commerce, the collision of thought and interest in a thousand ways unknown to other generations, have roused the popular mind from its former lethargy. It is awake, susceptible, quick to apprehend. Instead of being wedded to the old, and prejudiced against the new, it is, perhaps even to a perilous degree, disposed to distrust the old and to crave and seize the new. In such a state of things, whatever is said or done with earnestness and power is sure to tell effectually. Seed sown, whatever it may be, is likely to come speedily to the harvest.

A second circumstance that goes to the same point is, that the present seems to be peculiarly a crisis in the history of nations and of mankind, on which great interests for the future are depending. There are such periods in individual life. How often a young man is seen to be brought, as it were, to a determining point for all his coming years! Within a short space he will settle and fix his principles, his character, his plan of life and action. A little influence on him then becomes a most momentous influence, because it may decide so much in relation to all his future history. Very much like this, I apprehend, is the present era in the progress of the world. It is true of the whole civilized world, to a great extent, it is eminently true in regard to our own country, that great issues for coming generations appear to be crowded into this period in which we live, to be decided, for better or for worse, within a comparatively limited time. The greatest and most vital questions in regard to education, to civil and religious rights and institutions, to government and laws, to philosophy, morals, and religion, have come up, in the general excitement of the day, for new and more thorough and searching discussion. These earnest discussions will settle, in our own case, right or wrong, things which will enter, as elements of life or death, the character and state of the mighty people that in the next and in succeeding centuries shall occupy and fill this land. To act now, therefore, is to act at the decisive moment,—as when a force comes into the field of battle just when the contest is the hottest, and victory is hanging in suspense! The greatest results may often be achieved, in such a special juncture, by doing what in ordinary circumstances might accomplish very little. We of the present generation may not only help to decide aright the great practical questions of our time, but we may see the effects of our influence to such an extent that we may be assured that victory inclines towards the right, and so be able to anticipate the thanks that grateful posterity will render us. It is a noble thing to live when not only a few leading persons, but every individual, in proportion to what he is, may act with great results, at least the beginnings and the certainty of which he may also himself be allowed to see. Life, at such a juncture, must be allowed to have a special value.

I will notice but one more feature of our time which stands in special relation to the present value of a life. I think we cannot be mistaken in affirming that never before was Christ, the Head of that divine kingdom which is to fill and transform the world, so manifestly as now bringing into effective action the great spiritual forces of that kingdom. I would not speak on this point in a vague and general manner. Let me explain precisely what I mean.

The view which divine revelation gives us, and which we as believers in that revelation take, in relation to the future of the world, is this: That Christ, as the Redeemer of the world, has an invisible and spiritual dominion over it and in it; that this kingdom essentially consists in the establishment of truth, and right, and love, as permanent and controlling forces, in the hearts of men; that it is the setting up of this kingdom that is to bring in that far better and happier period of the world—that golden age—for which humanity is sighing, and to which the hopes of the human race continually go forward; and that, for the evolution of the powers and influences of this kingdom, Christ has from the day of his ascension been administering the providential government of the world. These, I say, to us are simple facts of revelation.

But it has never been the method of Providence to lead on faster than mankind, or at least the most advanced portion of mankind, were able to follow. It has plainly been the purpose of Christ to bring in his reign in such a way as at once to help on and to keep pace with the culture and progress of the race. As he said to the disciples, "I have many things to say unto you, but ye cannot bear them *now*," even so in effect he has been saying to the people of past centuries, I have many works to do, many spiritual forces to reveal, in the moral regeneration of the world, but ye are not ready for them yet. So the day of his special power has lingered. Things have progressed, sometimes with powerful impulses, yet the general progress has seemed slow. Good men have lived, and laboured, and suffered—have prayed, and waited, and died—sustained by steady faith, without having seen the signs of the coming of the Son of man with power.

But consider what has happened within the present century, by which the powerful coming of Christ to set up his reign is seen. The last century closed with two great acts—the achievement of American freedom, which was as the rising of a day star to the nations; and the dreadful tragedy of the French Revolution; and these, with the subsequent career of the first French emperor, so shattered the old foundations of tyranny in Europe and America, that the whole structure has tottered ever since, and cannot be made secure. Oppression may linger for some time longer, in the shape of governmental despotism or of domestic slavery; but He who comes to preach deliverance to the captive, and the opening of the prison doors to them that are bound, has given it the death-blow. *Die it must and will*, in spite of all the commercial and political doctors in the world. It is a question of mere time.

At the opening of this century, Christ, who is the Life, wrought in his Church the beginnings of a new spiritual vitality, the fruit of which was a waking up to the great duty of carrying the blessings of Christianity to every creature. So was inaugurated the missionary work which is never to cease till not only the mountain-tops of the long benighted lands shall all be gilded by the beams of the Sun of righteousness, but even the lowliest valleys shall be flooded with his light.

The Holy Scriptures, which testify of Christ, embody his teachings, reveal immortality, redemption, and eternal retribution, and which are one of the great moral instrumentalities of his kingdom, in connection chiefly with the missionary work, he has caused to be translated into more than a hundred and fifty tongues, including all the most important languages of men. So He who is to reign is applying his truth to the universal heart of humanity.

Finally, the Holy Spirit, the highest and most wonderful and effective force of the spiritual kingdom of Christ, and which it is given him to dispense, he has poured out, within this century, to an extent and with a power of operation which has put cavillers to silence, and given even the great body of believers a new conception altogether as to the part he has to do in bringing the world to its coming day of joy.

What impressive illustrations of the power of Christ in the dispensation of the Spirit, and of his grace in bestowing pardon and peace with God, have the last two or three years afforded in all parts of our country! What age before has ever witnessed such? Wonders of a similar kind are now occurring in long-afflicted Ireland, and even in staid and unimpulsive Scotland herself. In England, too, the good work is now begun; and in Norway and Sweden it is going on with power. Christian life, Christian unity in spirit, Christian philanthropy and love, Christian activity and zeal—these are the blessed fruits of the Holy Spirit's work.

In these and other similar things, which must be traced directly to the power and grace of Christ, as the Head of the kingdom of God among mankind, we not only find the proof that he is more than ever revealing himself as intent on subduing the world unto himself, but we find also the ground of reasonable expectation that he is now going on to make, comparatively, a short work on the earth. We seem to see him come at last, in the fulness of time, to work mightily in his people, and, as it were, to put himself at their head for the speedy conquest and moral purification of the world. Whether, therefore, we think of the privilege of *seeing* all these glorious revelations of Christ's agency and headship, or of the honour and the happiness of being permitted for years to co-operate with him in the great movements he is starting, a life at such a time must have a special value—a value, as compared with a life lived in other periods of the world, beyond all computation. Blessed, indeed, are the eyes that see the things that *we* see, and that hear the things that we hear—far, far beyond the blessedness of those who lived when Christ was on the earth, or at any other time before or since his coming.

Let us pause, then, at this point, for time will not allow us to prolong our necessarily imperfect sketch of the striking features of our day—let us pause and deliberately estimate, each one, as an individual, the value of a life at such an era. Quite probably, we have not seriously considered it. It is, indeed, exceedingly difficult to appreciate it fully. We can only approximate the truth by dwelling distinctly on the fact, that, as regards the means of improving to the utmost all our capacities; the liberty of acting as we will, with unlimited room for choice; the opportunity to labour with the highest effectiveness to accomplish something worthy and to make our mark upon the world; and the privilege of feeling that, more sensibly than any before us ever could have done, we are entering into the decisive movements of Jesus Christ for the recovery of the world to truth, and righteousness, and love —it is only, I say, by dwelling on the fact that in all these things we have a vast advantage over those who have lived before us, that we can come in any good degree to comprehend the real worth of this short life which it is given us to live—which we *are* living, in these auspicious circumstances. How incalculable the loss to us, if we so fail to reflect on our position as that we do *not* comprehend the truth!

For what that is admirable in character, that is right and noble in action, that is glorious in achievement, and honourable and blessed in active sympathy with Christ, is not within *our* reach? We may, certainly, even in our favourable circumstances, live to but very little purpose. We may live selfishly, pursuing mean and unworthy ends, to make a little show, to hoard up wealth with greediness, to chase any of the vain shadows of earthly and sensual good. But if we know the worth of life, and act accordingly, what may not we who are alive at this day, or some of us, become before we die? What energy of virtuous action, what beautiful examples of well-doing, in the various spheres of duty, may we not exhibit to the world? What may we not, in part or whole, accomplish, in which we and others may rejoice, and for which this and other times will cherish and bless our memories? What wondrous changes in the condition of the world, involving the vastly augmented welfare of our race, may we not see wrought out by Christ, and in part through our own instrumentality, before our sun of life shall set?

These questions may be appropriately put to all in every assembly. They have, however, special force as addressed to those who are yet young. You, my young friends, some of you may live to see the close of the present century; and if the forty years last past have wrought such changes, the forty that shall follow will, with the greatest probability, bring others still more wonderful. The year 1900 will see the population of our country spreading from the one ocean to the other. It will see us, if a united people, and still smiled upon by Providence, the most powerful people on the globe. It will see the institution of slavery hasting to its end, if not destroyed. It will see the power of Christianity in this land and in the world prodigiously augmented. It will see the hopes of humanity far brighter, as the prospects of the future will be far more bright and cheering, than they have ever been before. O young man, young woman, that may live to reach that date, will it not then seem to you to have been a thing sublime and blessed to have not only lived in the midst of such events, but also to have borne in them some earnest, high, and honourable part! Yes, yes, it will; believe it, and wake now fully and finally to the *inexpressible value of a life* in such a time as this in which it is given you to live! But most of us now here will have closed our mortal course long before the last sands of this century run out. It is for us to make the most of every moment that remains.

Let me only say, in closing, that with the thought of the divine goodness, in permitting us to live in such a period, we may quicken our gratitude to-day. While with a thousand tender and pleasant recollections we offer thanks to Almighty God, while in our families our hearts are gladdened with influences of cheerfulness and love, let us reflect how widely different had been our lot in any of the centuries gone by. For all the good and hopeful things that it is now given our eyes to see and our ears to hear, for everything that enhances the value of a life in this our native land, and in this our most momentous era, let us render hearty thanksgiving to our God. May his Spirit so touch our hearts as to call forth from them that genuine gratitude which is "the perfume of the soul!" May he give us some just sense of our high responsibility, and kindle in our souls such Christian aspirations, such lofty purposes, such firm resolves to make the utmost of our lives, that, having given our years to Christ, and done our utmost in his service, we may go to our graves at last as the summer sun goes down serenely to his setting, and keep an eternal thanksgiving with the Church of the redeemed amidst the splendours of his throne!*

* The above discourse was delivered on occasion of the Annual Thanksgiving.

www.ingramcontent.com/pod-product-compliance
Lightning Source LLC
LaVergne TN
LVHW010237110826
845151LV00004B/1322
* 9 7 8 1 4 2 5 5 2 4 0 5 0 *